978-3949070 174
AF609163

**"Always just a handful of words –
but they open up a whole world every time."**

Smudo (about Songspiration)

Scan the Spotify codes to play every song instantly!

1.

Click the search bar in your Spotify app.
Then tip the camera icon at the top right.

2.

Scan the printed Spotify
code on the calendar page.

3.

Enjoy the music!

Music was my first Love & it will be my Last

1

JANUARY

SONG
Music Was My First Love
ARTIST
John Miles
YEAR
1976

SONGSPIRATION CONTEXT

Happy New Year!
In 153 B.C., Roman consuls started beginning their year in office on January 1. But over 40,000 years ago, humans started listening to man-made music (from bone flutes).

FEATURED FONTS

Each created in the year of the song release (from top to bottom, left to right)

Bogart

Classified and available through identifont.com

Design: i_dbuero × Carsten Güth

GOOD TIMES NEVER SEEMED SO GOOD

JANUARY

SONG
Sweet Caroline
ARTIST
Neil Diamond
YEAR
1969

SONGSPIRATION CONTEXT

According to Neil Diamond, this song was divinely inspired. "I think there's a little bit of God in that song. I always have felt that," he told the *Los Angeles Times*. "There's no accounting for what can happen to a song."

FEATURED FONTS

Each created in the year of the song release (from top to bottom, left to right)

Didot

Classified and available through identifont.com

Design: i_dbuero × Sabine Schneider

What you gonna do with your LIFE?

JANUARY

SONG

Girls Just Want to Have Fun

ARTIST

Cyndi Lauper

YEAR

1983

SONGSPIRATION CONTEXT

Never forget: you always have several chances in life. The same can be said for this song, which has charted on the 'Hot 100' across three decades following its initial entry in 1983. Cyndi Lauper remade it as 'Hey Now (Girls Just Want to Have Fun)', peaking at #87 in 1995. Sixteen years later, the cast of *Glee* took its version to #59. Finally, in 2015 *the Voice* contestant Madi Davis reached #98 with her ethereal cover after she performed it on the TV show.

FEATURED FONTS

Each created in the year of the song release (from top to bottom, left to right)

Litera, Motter Corpus

Classified and available through identifont.com

Design: i_dbuero × Evelyn Binder

TAKE ME TO THAT OTHER PLACE

4

JANUARY

SONG
Beautiful Day
ARTIST
U2
YEAR
2000

SONGSPIRATION CONTEXT

The lyrics were inspired by Bono's experience with 'Jubilee 2000', a benefit urging politicians to cancel third world debt. Bono describes the song as being about "a man who has lost everything, but finds joy in what he still has."

FEATURED FONTS

Each created in the year of the song release (from top to bottom, left to right)

BorgstrandPro

Classified and available through identifont.com

Design: i_dbuero × Evelyn Binder

I just
I just
can't get
can't get
enough
enough

SONG
Just Can't Get Enough
ARTIST
Depeche Mode
YEAR
1981

SONGSPIRATION CONTEXT

Vince Clarke had just turned 20 when he penned this song, which turned out to be the last one he wrote for Depeche Mode. He left the band after the 'speak and Spell' album was released ... maybe he had just got enough.

FEATURED FONTS

Each created in the year of the song release (from top to bottom, left to right)

Aja, ITC Barcelona

Classified and available through identifont.com

Design: i_dbuero × Carsten Güth

MY SWEET LORD

JANUARY

SONG
My Sweet Lord
ARTIST
George Harrison
YEAR
1970

SONGSPIRATION CONTEXT

Today is Epiphany.
During a flight from Los Angeles to New York in 1971, Harrison's plane was hit by lightning, causing severe turbulence. He recalled chanting the 'hare krishna' mantra, which he credited with saving his life. Speaking with the Indian magazine 'Back to Godhead' in 1982, he said: "I know for me, the difference between making it and not making it was actually chanting the mantra." (songfacts.com)

FEATURED FONTS

Each created in the year of the song release (from top to bottom, left to right)
Avantgarde

Classified and available through identifont.com

Design: i_dbuero × Anja Osterwalder

c o m e
light my fire
o n
b a b y

SONG
Light My Fire

ARTIST
The Doors

YEAR
1967

SONGSPIRATION CONTEXT

"Jim [Morrison] had been writing all the songs and then one day we realized we didn't have enough tunes, so he said, "Hey, why don't you guys try and write songs?" I wrote 'Light My Fire' that night and brought it to the next rehearsal ... It's always kind of bugged me that so many people don't know I was the composer."
(Robby Krieger, guitarist)

FEATURED FONTS

Each created in the year of the song release (from top to bottom, left to right)

Amelia

Classified and available through identifont.com

Design: i_dbuero × OA Krimmel

CLAP ALONG if you feel like a ROOM without a ROOF

SONG
Happy
ARTIST
Pharrell Williams
YEAR
2013

SONGSPIRATION CONTEXT

Happy birthday, Pharrell! (born in1973) The song's video is the world's first-ever 24-hour music video. The visual plays on an all-day loop and follows more than 400 different characters enjoying daily bliss. Besides Pharrell Williams, the following stars are happy in it: Tyler, The Creator, Kelly Osbourne, Sérgio Mendes, Ana Ortiz, Magic Johnson, Jimmy Kimmel, Steve Martin and many more. And naturally the Minions pop up in the video that is the theme song for their film.

FEATURED FONTS

Each created in the year of the song release (from top to bottom, left to right)

Hermes, Fraktur, Mark Pro

Classified and available through identifont.com

Design: i_dbuero × Carsten Güth

Get the most exclusive, handmade oak stand for your calendar.

www.seltmannpublishers.com

Worldwide shipping, free within Germany

But you know
that when the
truth is told
That you can
get what you want
Or you can
just get old

SONG

Vienna

ARTIST

Billy Joel

YEAR

1977

SONGSPIRATION CONTEXT

For this song, Billy Joel was inspired by the city of Vienna and his father, a Holocaust survivor who lived there. Joel has explained that Vienna is a metaphor for old age, but subconsciously it could also be about his father himself.

FEATURED FONTS

Each created in the year of the song release (from top to bottom, left to right)

Harlow

Classified and available through identifont.com

Design: i_dbuero × OA Krimmel

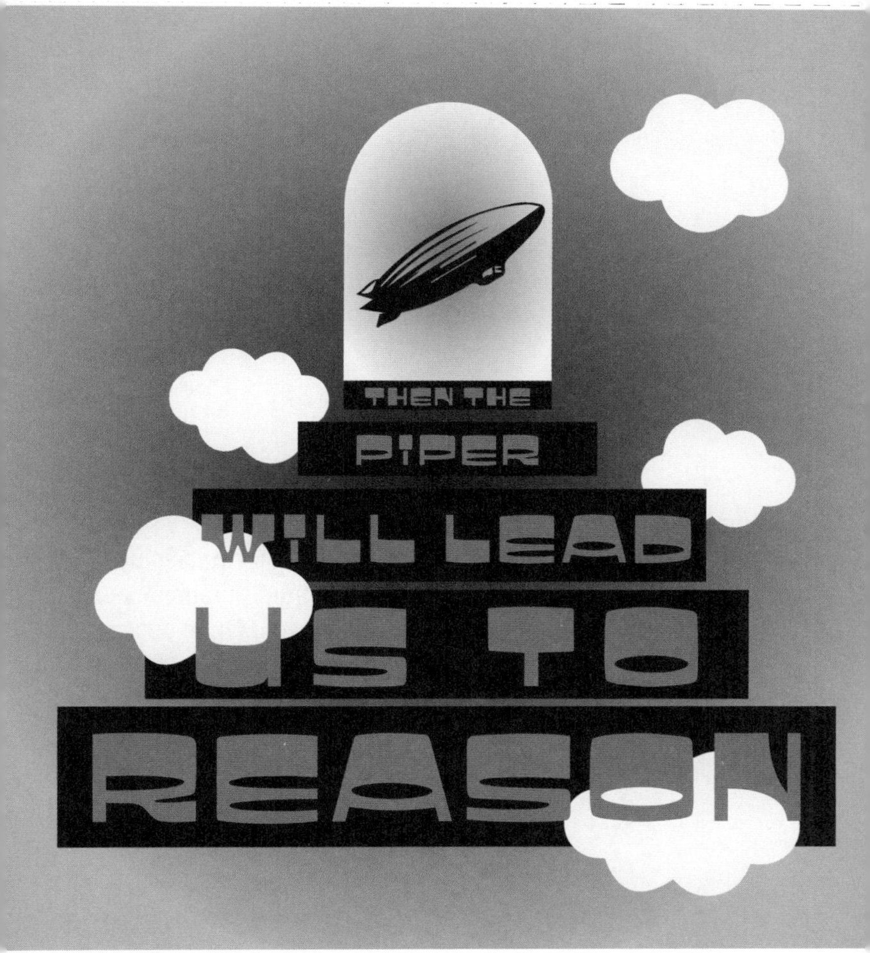

THEN THE PIPER WILL LEAD US TO REASON

JANUARY

SONG
Stairway to Heaven
ARTIST
Led Zeppelin
YEAR
1971

SONGSPIRATION CONTEXT

It is one of the most popular songs in the world. It also contains an outstanding guitar solo. While perhaps not as well known, the opening of the song includes a very succinct part played on the recorder. And since today is Recorder Day, we want to celebrate with this song.

FEATURED FONTS

Each created in the year of the song release (from top to bottom, left to right)

Jackson MN

Classified and available through identifont.com

Design: i_dbuero × Sabine Schneider

Every pure intention ends when the good times start

SONG
Bad Habits
ARTIST
Ed Sheeran
YEAR
2021

SONGSPIRATION CONTEXT

That's the way it is with good New Year's resolutions. The bad habits often prevail. But don't worry, others don't fare much better. And remember: tomorrow is the first new blank page in the book that is your life (or at least a new SONGSPIRATION motto).

FEATURED FONTS

Each created in the year of the song release (from top to bottom, left to right)

Asgard

Classified and available through identifont.com

Design: i_dbuero × Carsten Güth

People say believe half of what you see

12

JANUARY

SONG
I Heard It Through the Grapevine

ARTIST
Marvin Gaye

YEAR
1968

SONGSPIRATION CONTEXT

On today's date in 1959, the Motown record label, officially known as Motown Record Company, L. P., was founded under the name Tamla Record Company by Berry Gordy in Detroit, Michigan. Thank you for the music, Berry!

FEATURED FONTS

Each created in the year of the song release (from top to bottom, left to right)

Revue BT, Hawthorn

Classified and available through identifont.com

Design: i_dbuero × Evelyn Binder

I CAN FLY MY FRIENDS

JANUARY

SONG
The Show Must Go On
ARTIST
Queen
YEAR
1991

SONGSPIRATION CONTEXT

'The Show Must Go On' was written by Queen guitarist Brian May while lead singer Freddie Mercury was coming to the end of his life due to AIDS. It turned out that this album would be the last official studio album with Mercury. But the show had to go on – and Queen are still touring 30 years later, to the great delight of their millions of fans.

FEATURED FONTS

Each created in the year of the song release (from top to bottom, left to right)

Broadband

Classified and available through identifont.com

Design: i_dbuero × Sabine Schneider

THEY TRIED TO MAKE ME GO TO

REHAB

I SAID

NO, NO, NO

SONG
Rehab
ARTIST
Amy Winehouse
YEAR
2007

SONGSPIRATION CONTEXT

"On 'Rehab' I was walking down the street with Mark Ronson, who produced my last album. I just sang the hook out loud ... I sang the whole line exactly as it is on the record! Mark laughed and asked me who wrote it because he liked it. I told him I had just made it up, but that it was true, and he encouraged me to turn it into a song, which took me five minutes ... It was about what my old management company wanted me to do." (Amy Winehouse)

FEATURED FONTS

Each created in the year of the song release (from top to bottom, left to right)

Meloriac, Darkheart

Classified and available through identifont.com

Design: i_dbuero × Carsten Güth

SILVER MAGIC
SHIPS YOU
CARRY
JUMPERS, COKE,
SWEET
MARY JANE

SONG
Sugar Man
ARTIST
Rodríguez
YEAR
1970

SONGSPIRATION CONTEXT

The absolutely unbelievable story of Sixto Díaz Rodríguez goes like this: a musician records two albums that flop in his home country, the USA. He becomes a construction worker and is completely unaware that his songs become mega hits in Australia and South Africa. Only many, many years later does he find out about it and then fills arenas all over the world with thousands of spectators. The film about his life was awarded an Oscar.

FEATURED FONTS

Each created in the year of the song release (from top to bottom, left to right)

ITC Ronda

Classified and available through identifont.com

Design: i_dbuero × Evelyn Binder

16

JANUARY

SONG
Music Is the Answer
ARTIST
Joe Goddard
YEAR
2017

SONGSPIRATION CONTEXT

Who could have thought up this beautiful sentence? In the original, it says, “Music is the answer to the mystery of life”. And, who would have thought it, it comes from none other than ... Arthur Schopenhauer. In January 1840 the famous philosopher published *On the Basis of Morality*.

FEATURED FONTS

Each created in the year of the song release (from top to bottom, left to right)

WIND VF Mirrored NE, NW, W

Classified and available through identifont.com

Design: i_dbuero × OA Krimmel

If I Can Make It There I'll Make It ANYWHERE

JANUARY

SONG
Theme from New York, New York
ARTIST
Frank Sinatra
YEAR
1977

SONGSPIRATION CONTEXT
The song was actually composed for Liza Minnelli and the musical *New York, New York*. But both more or less flopped. Obviously *they couldn't make it there*! However Frank Sinatra's wife persuaded him one day to cover the song. Actually *he could make it there* and it became his signature hit, which remained in his repertoire until his last performances in 1994.

FEATURED FONTS
Each created in the year of the song release (from top to bottom, left to right)

Garamond

Classified and available through identifont.com

Design: i_dbuero × OA Krimmel

AND WHEN YOU SMILE THE WHOLE WORLD STOPS AND STARES FOR A WHILE

SONG
Just the Way You Are

ARTIST
Bruno Mars

YEAR
2010

SONGSPIRATION CONTEXT
"I'm a big fan of simple songs. When we wrote 'Just the Way You Are', I wasn't thinking of anything deep or poetic. I was telling a story. Get ready to fall in love!"
(Bruno Mars)

FEATURED FONTS
Each created in the year of the song release (from top to bottom, left to right)

Acier BAT

Classified and available through identifont.com

Design: i_dbuero × Carsten Güth

Yesterday
all my troubles
seemed so
far away

19

January

SONG
Yesterday
ARTIST
The Beatles
YEAR
1965

SONGSPIRATION CONTEXT
At this very moment, while you are reading these words, 'Yesterday' is playing on thousands of devices and encouraging its listeners to sing along. The song is the most covered pop song of all time. According to the *Guinness Book of Records* there are over 3,000 versions. For years, it was also the song with the most radio plays worldwide.

FEATURED FONTS
Each created in the year of the song release (from top to bottom, left to right)

Davida BT, Impact

Classified and available through identifont.com

Design: i_dbuero × Sabine Schneider

I'D TRADE ALL MY TOMORROWS
FOR ONE SINGLE YESTERDAY

SONG
Me and Bobby McGee

ARTIST
Janis Joplin

YEAR
1971

SONGSPIRATION CONTEXT

Janis Joplin died of a heroin overdose in 1970, at the age of 27, with the dubious privilege of entering the '27 Club'. Her album *Pearl*, was released in January 1971, just over three months after her death. It reached number one on the Billboard charts. She was posthumously inducted into the *Rock and Roll Hall of Fame* in 1995.

FEATURED FONTS

Each created in the year of the song release (from top to bottom, left to right)

Spadina

Classified and available through identifont.com

Design: i_dbuero × Sabine Schneider

won't you
take me to

FUNKY
TOWN

SONG
Funkytown
ARTIST
Lipps, Inc
YEAR
1979

SONGSPIRATION CONTEXT

'Funkytown' expresses a simple, repetitive yearning for the pulse of a bigger city, goosed by a killer ten-note synth riff. "Gotta make a move to a town that's right for me," sings Cynthia Johnson in a robotic, vocoderised voice (a precursor to the Auto-Tune sound) before busting out an unmodified, soulful wail. Released in 1979, 'Funkytown' came late to the disco party, but gave it a jolt of electricity. (Time Out)

FEATURED FONTS

Each created in the year of the song release (from top to bottom, left to right)

Brighton Plain, VAG Rounded

Classified and available through identifont.com

Design: i_dbuero × Evelyn Binder

Ready

* or *

~ not

here i

come ~

SONG
Ready or Not
ARTIST
Fugees
YEAR
1997

SONGSPIRATION CONTEXT

"I believe there will be a day when the Fugees get together, but everyone in the group's gotta be ready. The Fugees are definitely going to get back together. The time will come. You've gotta wait, man." (Wyclef Jean, 2011)

FEATURED FONTS

Each created in the year of the song release (from top to bottom, left to right)

Jive Talk, Youbee, Klepto ITC

Classified and available through identifont.com

Design: i_dbuero × Carsten Güth

FRIDAY

I'm in

JANUARY

SONG
Friday I'm in Love
ARTIST
The Cure
YEAR
1992

SONGSPIRATION CONTEXT

"When we started I wasn't the singer.
I was the drunk rhythm guitarist, who wrote
all these weird songs."
(Robert Smith)

FEATURED FONTS

Each created in the year of the song release (from top to bottom, left to right)

FF Blur, Hobo, Darkside

Classified and available through
identifont.com

Design: i_dbuero × Carsten Güth

AIN'T GOT NOTHING *but* love *babe*

8

DAYS A WEEK

SONG
Eight Days a Week
ARTIST
The Beatles
YEAR
1964

SONGSPIRATION CONTEXT

There are two stories about where the title came from. In Bob Spitz' *The Beatles: The Biography*, Paul McCartney claims that he asked his chauffeur (while being driven to John's house in Weybridge) if he was busy, and got the answer "Busy? I've been working eight days a week." In a later interview, Paul says that it was Ringo who coined the phrase: "He said it as though he were an overworked chauffeur. When we heard it, we said 'Really?' Bing! Got it!" John Lennon also claimed it was one of Ringo's malapropisms. (songfacts.com)

FEATURED FONTS

Each created in the year of the song release (from top to bottom, left to right)

Miedinger, Sabon

Classified and available through identifont.com

Design: i_dbuero × Carsten Güth

Hello,
Hello,
Hello,

How low!

SONG
Smells Like Teen Spirit
ARTIST
Nirvana
YEAR
1991

SONGSPIRATION CONTEXT

The song title derives from a phrase written on Cobain's wall by his friend Kathleen Hanna, singer of the band *Bikini Kill*: "Kurt smells like Teen Spirit." Hanna meant that Cobain smelled like the deodorant *Teen Spirit*, which she and Tobi Vail, his then-girlfriend, had discovered during a trip to the grocery store. Cobain was unaware of the deodorant, he had interpreted it as a revolutionary slogan, as they had been discussing anarchism and punk rock. (via abc.net)

FEATURED FONTS

Each created in the year of the song release (from top to bottom, left to right)

FF Blur

Classified and available through identifont.com

Design: i_dbuero × Carsten Güth

I cross the ocean for a

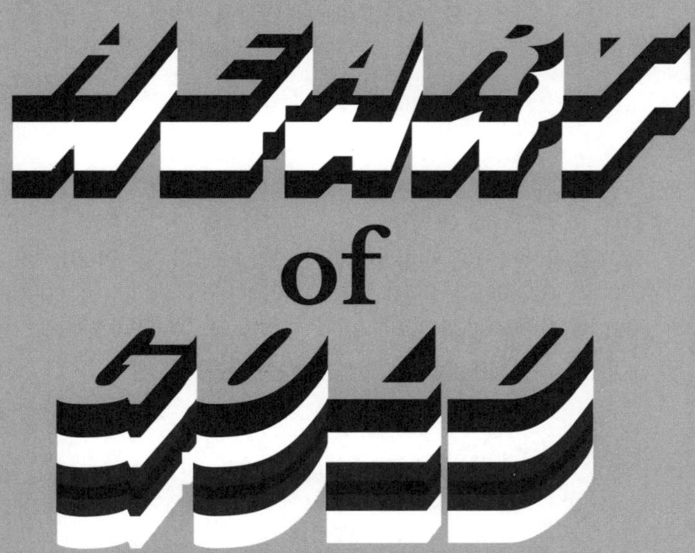

26

JANUARY

SONG
Heart of Gold
ARTIST
Neil Young
YEAR
1972

SONGSPIRATION CONTEXT

'Hearts of gold' are rare to find. A golden favourite of the SONGSPIRATION team: the *Heart of Gold* spaceship, which was the first to use the Infinite Improbability Drive (according to Douglas Adams' *The Hitchhiker's Guide to the Galaxy*). And it stands to reason that Adams was probably inspired by this song to name this spaceship.

FEATURED FONTS

Each created in the year of the song release (from top to bottom, left to right)

Libre Baskerville, Buster

Classified and available through identifont.com

Design: i_dbuero × Carsten Güth

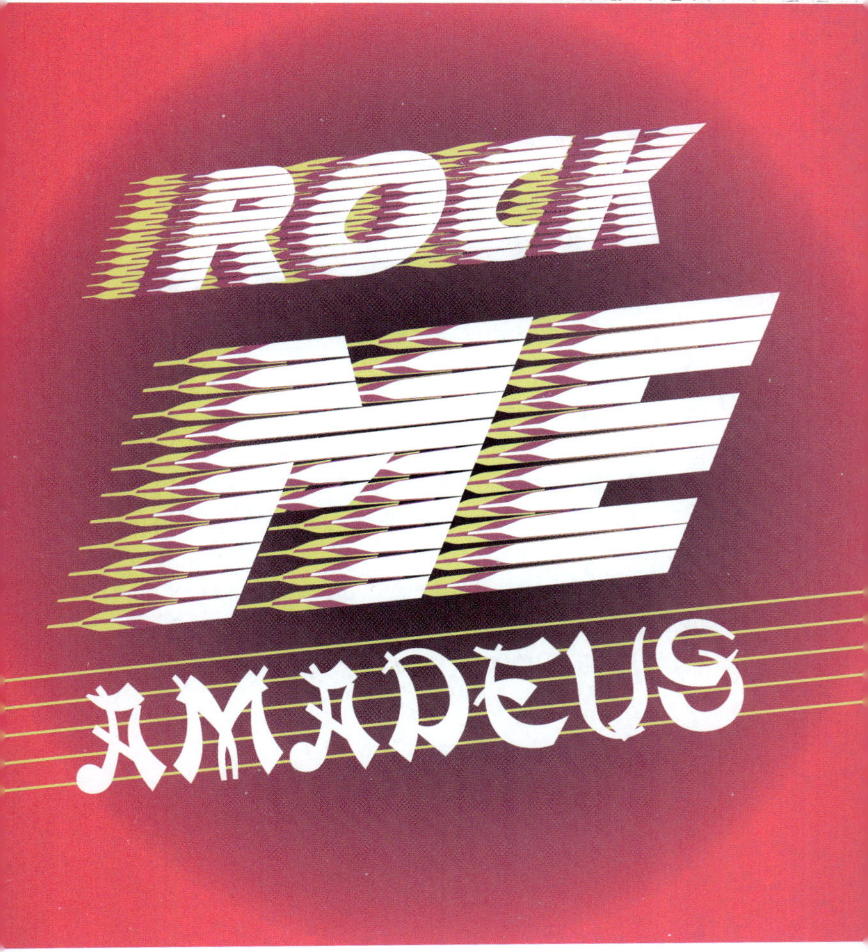

ROCK ME AMADEUS

JANUARY

SONG
Rock Me Amadeus
ARTIST
Falco
YEAR
1985

SONGSPIRATION CONTEXT

It's not often that a non-English language song turns into a huge international hit – in German with an Austrian accent, it's probably only ever happened once. Falco rapped about the genius Mozart, as if he had been some kind of primal punk rocker. But if you know that Mozart also composed a 6-part canon entitled 'Lick Me in the Arse', then you can definitely agree with Falco here. Mozart was born on January 27, 1756.

FEATURED FONTS

Each created in the year of the song release (from top to bottom, left to right)

Slipstream, Mandarin

Classified and available through identifont.com

Design: i_dbuero × OA Krimmel

First born

UNICORN

HARD

CORE

SOFTPORN

SONG
Californication
ARTIST
Red Hot Chili Peppers
YEAR
1999

SONGSPIRATION CONTEXT

The song title is a combination of 'California' and 'fornication'. This neologism has been used since the 1950s to describe the "haphazard, unthinking population expansion in the arid regions of Southern California." The text grapples with the moral and cultural decline of the Western world. California, and Hollywood in particular, was chosen as a prime example.

FEATURED FONTS

Each created in the year of the song release (from top to bottom, left to right)

Arial Black

Classified and available through identifont.com

Design: i_dbuero × Carsten Güth

MAN
IN THE
ICE CREAM VAN

SONG
Weekend
ARTIST
Scooter
YEAR
2003

SONGSPIRATION CONTEXT

Would you like some more song wisdom from Scooter? Gladly: "It's nice to be important, but it's more important to be nice." or "The Question is What is the Question?" and another important question: "How much is the Fish?". Finally don't forget to remember: "Don't throw away the banana boxes" – "Hyper Hyper", isn't it?!

FEATURED FONTS

Each created in the year of the song release (from top to bottom, left to right)

Rodeo, Avenir Next

Classified and available through identifont.com

Design: i_dbuero × Carsten Güth

I am
Human
&
I need to be
Loved

SONG
How Soon Is Now?
ARTIST
The Smiths
YEAR
1984

SONGSPIRATION CONTEXT

"I wanted it to be really, really tense and swampy, all at the same time. Layering the slide part was what gave it the real tension. The tremolo effect came from laying down a regular rhythm part with a capo at the 2nd fret on a Les Paul, then sending that out into the live room to four Fender Twins. John was controlling the tremolo on two of them and I was controlling the other two, and whenever they went out of sync, we just had to stop the track and start all over again. It took an eternity." (Johnny Marr, guitarist)

FEATURED FONTS

Each created in the year of the song release (from top to bottom, left to right)

Eclat, Litera

Classified and available through identifont.com

Design: i_dbuero × Carsten Güth

COME AS YOU ARE AS YOU WERE

SONG
Come as You Are
ARTIST
Nirvana
YEAR
1991

SONGSPIRATION CONTEXT

Kurt Cobain's hometown Aberdeen added the words "Come as You Are" to the inscription on their town signs in 2005. This was an initiative of the 'Kurt Cobain Memorial Committee', which built a memorial park and youth centre in the city. This was seen by some as bitter irony, as Cobain expressed his dislike of the city throughout his life.

FEATURED FONTS

Each created in the year of the song release (from top to bottom, left to right)

MetaCorrespondence, Felix Titling

Classified and available through identifont.com

Design: i_dbuero × Sabine Schneider

When you're SMILIN'…

The whole world smiles with you

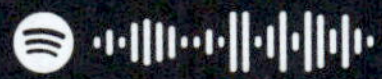

1

FEBRUARY

SONG
When You’re Smiling (The Whole World Smiles With You)

ARTIST
Louis Armstrong

YEAR
1928 (Armstrong versions 1929/1956)

SONGSPIRATION CONTEXT
This song has been covered by Frank Sinatra, Nat King Cole, Roberta Flack, Shirley Bassey, Dean Martin, Louis Prima, The Duke Ellington Orchestra, Doris Day, Judy Garland, Big Kahuna and The Copa Cat Pack, Andy Williams, Fats Domino, Michael Bublé, The Ukulele Orchestra of Great Britain as well as hundreds of other certainly-smiling-while-singing artists …
That says it all.

FEATURED FONTS
Each created in the year of the song release (from top to bottom, left to right)

Parisian

Classified and available through identifont.com

Design: i_dbuero × Sabine Schneider

I
got
you
babe

SONG
I Got You Babe
ARTIST
Sonny & Cher
YEAR
1965

SONGSPIRATION CONTEXT

"OK campers, rise and shine! – and don't forget your booties 'cause it's cooooooold out there today".
"It's cold out there every day. What is this, Miami Beach?"
Getting déjà vu? The song and the matching quote are from the movie *Groundhog Day*. And that's what day it is today – like every year: Groundhog Day!

FEATURED FONTS

Each created in the year of the song release (from top to bottom, left to right)

P22 Zebra

Classified and available through identifont.com

Design: i_dbuero × Carsten Güth

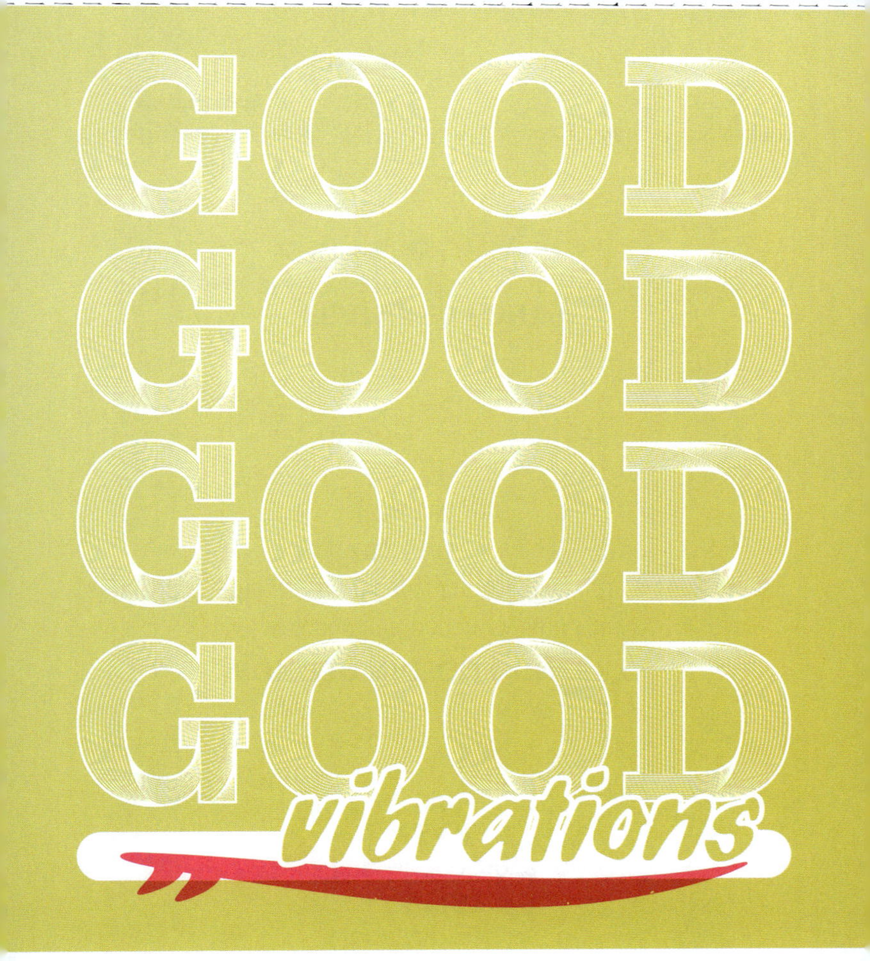

GOOD GOOD GOOD GOOD vibrations

FEBRUARY

SONG
Good Vibrations
ARTIST
The Beach Boys
YEAR
1966

SONGSPIRATION CONTEXT

"I wake up in the morning and I say
'Ahh! Today's the day for a song! I'm going to write a song today!'
And I do. I write a song."
(Brian Wilson)

FEATURED FONTS

Each created in the year of the song release (from top to bottom, left to right)

Serifa Black, Ecsetiras

Classified and available through identifont.com

Design: i_dbuero × Martin Drozmann

FEBRUARY

SONG
This Is the Day
ARTIST
The The
YEAR
1983

SONGSPIRATION CONTEXT

To call The The a band in the conventional sense would not do justice to founder Matt Johnson's ideas. He prefers a loose network of musicians to a permanent line-up. More than 300 musicians, including Marc Almond, Neneh Cherry, Sinead O'Connor or The Smiths guitarist Johnny Marr have accompanied him live or in the studio since 1979. And *this is not the day* to stop yet. He is still touring in the 2020s.

FEATURED FONTS

Each created in the year of the song release (from top to bottom, left to right)

Motter Corpus, Chromium

Classified and available through identifont.com

Design: i_dbuero × OA Krimmel

I SAID A HIP-HOP, THE HIPPIE THE HIPPIE / TO THE HIP, HIP HOP YOU DON'T STOP

FEBRUARY

SONG
Rapper's Delight
ARTIST
The Sugarhill Gang
YEAR
1979

SONGSPIRATION CONTEXT

A hit that truly made music history – it was the first rap song ever to make it into the American Hot 100. And strictly speaking, that was still in the 70s, because the single was released in the USA in September 1979. They used the Fatback Band sample without permission, of course, because that was not yet regulated. Another beat is from Chic's 'Good Times' – here the hip-hoppers weren't even the first: Queen had already used it on 'Another One Bites the Dust'.

FEATURED FONTS

Each created in the year of the song release (from top to bottom, left to right)

Milka (dry)

Classified and available through identifont.com

Design: i_dbuero × Tim Oliver Schweizer

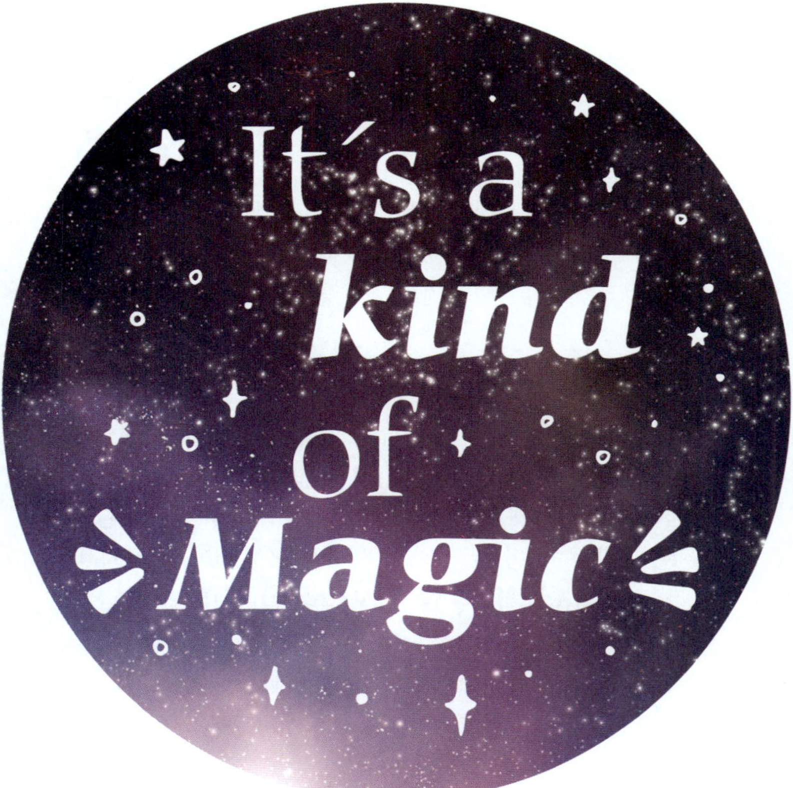

It´s a
kind
of
Magic

FEBRUARY

SONG
A Kind of Magic
ARTIST
Queen
YEAR
1986

SONGSPIRATION CONTEXT

On 6 February 1952, King George VI died, making Elizabeth II the new Queen. This was a *kind of magic* that led to the Queen also becoming the longest-reigning Britisch monarch and the longest-reigning female monarch in history. She reigned until 2022.

FEATURED FONTS

Each created in the year of the song release (from top to bottom, left to right)

Carmina BT

Classified and available through identifont.com

Design: i_dbuero × Ralph Rieker

And in the end

The love you take

Is equal to

the love you make

SONG
The End
ARTIST
The Beatles
YEAR
1969

SONGSPIRATION CONTEXT

February 7, 1964: The Beatles landed at New York's John F. Kennedy Airport for their first American tour. They were also guests on the *Ed Sullivan Show*. Around 73 million Americans watched, a record in television history at the time. Their phenomenal global career now really took off...

FEATURED FONTS

Each created in the year of the song release (from top to bottom, left to right)

Wonderbrush, Didoni

Classified and available through identifont.com

Design: i_dbuero × Carsten Güth

DESPITE ALL
MY RAGE
I AM STILL JUST
A RAT
IN A CAGE

SONG
Bullet with Butterfly Wings
ARTIST
The Smashing Pumpkins
YEAR
1995

SONGSPIRATION CONTEXT

"I was sitting there bored out of my mind, they [the producers] were dicking around with some microphone, and I had this line in my head, 'Despite all my rage. I'm still just a rat in a cage.' I was just sitting there, bored, and I picked up the guitar and I started singing. But what if the guy had been like, 'Ooh we're ready!'? People don't appreciate that there's a thing that needs to happen. The stars need to align." (Billy Corgan)

FEATURED FONTS

Each created in the year of the song release (from top to bottom, left to right)

P22 DeStijl Tall

Classified and available through identifont.com

Design: i_dbuero × Daniel Bognár aka damentennis.com

ti amo

FEBRUARY

SONG
Ti Amo

ARTIST
Umberto Tozzi

YEAR
1995

SONGSPIRATION CONTEXT

“Unless you are a pizza, the answer is yes,
I can live without you.” (Bill Murray)
Today is World Pizza Day.

FEATURED FONTS

Each created in the year of the song release (from top to bottom, left to right)

Helvetica

Classified and available through
identifont.com

Design: i_dbuero × Anja Osterwalder

I'm starting with the man in the mirror

SONG
Man in the Mirror
ARTIST
Michael Jackson
YEAR
1987

SONGSPIRATION CONTEXT

“A star can never die. It just turns into a smile and melts back into the cosmic music, the dance of life.”
(Michael Jackson)

FEATURED FONTS

Each created in the year of the song release (from top to bottom, left to right)

Gerstner BQ

Classified and available through identifont.com

Design: i_dbuero × Sabine Schneider

THERE'S A STARMAN WAITING IN THE SKY

FEBRUARY

SONG
Starman
ARTIST
David Bowie
YEAR
1972

SONGSPIRATION CONTEXT

"I love 'Starman' as it's the concept of hope that the song communicates. That 'we're not alone' and 'they' contact the kids, not the adults, and kind of say 'get on with it.' 'Let the children boogie' music and rock 'n' roll! It lifted the attention away from the depressing affairs in the '70s, made the future look better. 'Starman' was the first Bowie song since 'Space Oddity' with mass appeal. After 'Starman' everything changed."
(Woody Woodmansey, drummer, 2008)

FEATURED FONTS

Each created in the year of the song release (from top to bottom, left to right)

Bottleneck

Classified and available through identifont.com

Design: i_dbuero × Sarah Grgic

HA-HA

SHAKE IT, SHAKE IT, SHAKE IT,

FEELGOOD

HA-HA

HA!

12

FEBRUARY

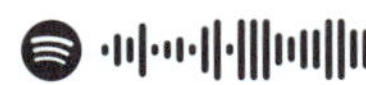

SONG
Feel Good Inc.
ARTIST
Gorillaz
YEAR
2005

SONGSPIRATION CONTEXT

Aside from appearing in the *Guinness Book of World Records* under 'Most Successful Virtual Band', the band broke another record at the timefor the most views on YouTube after the release of their music video, 'Stylo', featuring Bruce Willis. The video garnered 900,000 views in the first 24 hours.

FEATURED FONTS

Each created in the year of the song release (from top to bottom, left to right)

Glass Jaw, Catseye

Classified and available through identifont.com

Design: i_dbuero × Syl Hillier

All we hear is

radio

GA GA

Radio

BLAH BLAH

SONG
Radio Gaga
ARTIST
Queen
YEAR
1984

SONGSPIRATION CONTEXT

Today is World Radio Day. Queen drummer Roger Taylor wrote the song back then, however, more as a criticism of the radio stations that played the same old boring songs all the time. *Fun fact*: Lady Gaga took her name from this song. Born Stefani Germanotta, she started using the moniker when she needed a stage name.

FEATURED FONTS

Each created in the year of the song release (from top to bottom, left to right)

Futura Round, Mundene Rock

Classified and available through identifont.com

Design: i_dbuero × Carsten Güth

You put the

BOOM

BOOM

into my

HEART

SONG
Wake Me Up Before You Go-Go

ARTIST
Wham!

YEAR
1984

SONGSPIRATION CONTEXT

Today is Valentine's Day! *Wake up and go-go* shopping flowers! By the way: Andrew Ridgeley from Wham! wanted to be woken up by his mother and wrote a note on his door: "Wake me up up", and when he realised that he had written one word twice, he ended the sentence with "before you go go". George Michael loved that and wrote the song called 'Wake Me Up Before You Go-Go'. It became Wham's first American hit.

FEATURED FONTS

Each created in the year of the song release (from top to bottom, left to right)

Paddington

Classified and available through identifont.com

Design: i_dbuero × Carsten Güth

1

Tell me 2

that you

love

3

me

more 4

SONG
1234
ARTIST
Feist
YEAR
2007

SONGSPIRATION CONTEXT

Galileo Galilei was born in Pisa on this day in 1564.
For the Inquisition of the Roman Catholic Church, he had to renounce his alleged heresies (the earth revolves around the sun, which Copernicus had already discovered). This was the only way he could save life and limb from death by fire. On the other hand, he had to sacrifice his beloved scientific beliefs.

FEATURED FONTS

Each created in the year of the song release (from top to bottom, left to right)

Bisque

Classified and available through identifont.com

Design: i_dbuero × Carsten Güth

Maybe you can
show me
how to love

SONG
Blinding Lights
ARTIST
The Weeknd
YEAR
2020

SONGSPIRATION CONTEXT

The Weeknd's real name is Abel Makkonen Tesfaye. After dropping out of high school at the age of 17, he came up with his stage name: "left one *weekend* and never came home". On Spotify, he surpassed a new record with 75 million listeners in one month, something only four artists before him had achieved. Abel was born on February 16, 1990 in Toronto.

FEATURED FONTS

Each created in the year of the song release (from top to bottom, left to right)

Grobek

Classified and available through identifont.com

Design: i_dbuero × Carsten Güth

MY WOMAN GIVES ME POWER

FEBRUARY

SONG
You Should Be Dancing
ARTIST
Bee Gees
YEAR
1976

SONGSPIRATION CONTEXT

Casting the role of John Travolta's dance partner in *Saturday Night Fever* proved difficult. Hundreds of women auditioned, but none seemed right. As fate would have it, Karen Gorney shared a taxi one day with a stranger who turned out to be the nephew of the film's producer. He mentioned that his uncle was working on a film, and Gorney replied, "Oh, am I in it?" – her standard joke whenever she heard about a film production. The nephew eventually suggested Gorney as a candidate, and the rest is history.

FEATURED FONTS

Each created in the year of the song release (from top to bottom, left to right)

Geometr885 BT

Classified and available through identifont.com

Design: i_dbuero × Evelyn Binder

Just get ready fi

SONG
Work
ARTIST
Rihanna ft. Drake
YEAR
2016

SONGSPIRATION CONTEXT

The hook line of the song features some words sung by Rihanna in Patois, a Jamaican dialect that is common throughout much of the Caribbean.
'Haffi' means 'have to' – 'Ah guh' means 'is going to' – 'Meh nuh cyar' means 'I don't care'.

FEATURED FONTS

Each created in the year of the song release (from top to bottom, left to right)

GT America

Classified and available through identifont.com

Design: i_dbuero × Carsten Güth

I never dreamed that I'd meet somebody like you

FEBRUARY

SONG
Wicked Game
ARTIST
Chris Isaak
YEAR
1990

SONGSPIRATION CONTEXT

Today in 1951 the actress Jane Seymour was born.
Even James Bond never dreamed that he'd meet her
as Solitaire in *Live and Let Die*.
But there was Voodoo in the game.

FEATURED FONTS

Each created in the year of the song release (from top to bottom, left to right)

Century Gothic, Cattlebrand

Classified and available through identifont.com

Design: i_dbuero × Katrin Schlüsener

and I never dreamed that I'd loose

somebody like you

SONG
Wicked Game
ARTIST
Chris Isaak
YEAR
1990

SONGSPIRATION CONTEXT

A person who made Hollywood history passed away in 2022: Sidney Poitier. Born on 20 February 1927 into a poor family, he made it as the first African-American actor to receive an Academy Award in 1964. He was an important role model for the following generations of self-confident Black Americans.

FEATURED FONTS

Each created in the year of the song release (from top to bottom, left to right)

Century Gothic, Cattlebrand

Classified and available through identifont.com

Design: i_dbuero × Katrin Schlüsener

we'll all
float
on
okay

SONG
Float On
ARTIST
Modest Mouse
YEAR
2004

SONGSPIRATION CONTEXT

In February 2004, the *Stardust* spacecraft made a close flyby of the comet *Wild-2*, collecting comet and interstellar dust in a substance called 'aerogel'.
Two years later, the samples made it back to Earth in a return capsule that landed in Utah's Great Salt Lake Desert.

FEATURED FONTS

Each created in the year of the song release (from top to bottom, left to right)

dubbeldik

Classified and available through identifont.com

Design: i_dbuero × Jan Hurni

We

in a

found

hopeless

love

place

♣♠♦♥

SONG
We Found Love
ARTIST
Rihanna
YEAR
2011

SONGSPIRATION CONTEXT

In 2008 former Prime Minister of Barbados, David Thompson, announced that there would be an annual 'Rihanna Day' every year on 22 February. Although this is not a bank holiday, people come together to celebrate it every year by listening to her music. Occasionally she even returns to perform. What's more, the street where she used to live has been renamed to 'Rihanna Drive'.

FEATURED FONTS

Each created in the year of the song release (from top to bottom, left to right)

Abril Fatface, Raleway

Classified and available through identifont.com

Design: i_dbuero × Evelyn Binder

23

FEBRUARY

SONG
Piano Man
ARTIST
Billy Joel
YEAR
1973

SONGSPIRATION CONTEXT

"I have no idea why that song became so popular. It's like a karaoke favorite. The melody is not very good and very repetitious, while the lyrics are like limericks. I was shocked and embarrassed when it became a hit. But my songs are like my kids, and I look at that song and think: 'My kid did pretty well.'"
(Billy Joel in an interview, 2006)

FEATURED FONTS

Each created in the year of the song release (from top to bottom, left to right)

Sol Heavy, Pierrot

Classified and available through identifont.com

Design: i_dbuero × Evelyn Binder

ONE PILL MAKES YOU

LARGER

& ONE PILL MAKES YOU

SMALL

SONG
White Rabbit
ARTIST
Jefferson Airplane
YEAR
1967

SONGSPIRATION CONTEXT

"I always felt like a good-looking school teacher singing 'White Rabbit'. I'd sing the words slowly and precisely, so the people who needed to hear them wouldn't miss the point. But they did. To this day, I don't think most people realize the song was aimed at parents who drank and told their kids not to do drugs. I felt they were full of shit, but to write a good song, you need a few more words than that." (Singer Grace Slick, *Anatomy of a Song*)

FEATURED FONTS

Each created in the year of the song release (from top to bottom, left to right)

Press Gothic

Classified and available through identifont.com

Design: i_dbuero × Carsten Güth

SING
WITH ME
SING
FOR THE YEAR
SING
FOR THE
LAUGHTER AND
SING
FOR THE TEAR

SONG
Dream On
ARTIST
Aerosmith
YEAR
1973

SONGSPIRATION CONTEXT

A breakthrough came for the sound of the band when Steven Tyler bought an RMI keyboard with money he found in a suitcase outside of where the band was staying. The 'suitcase incident' became part of Aerosmith lore, as Tyler didn't tell his bandmates that he took the money, and when gangsters came looking for it, he continued to play dumb. (songfacts.com)

FEATURED FONTS

Each created in the year of the song release (from top to bottom, left to right)

Sol Pro

Classified and available through identifont.com

Design: i_dbuero × Evelyn Binder

Jump around!

JUMP AROUND! ♲ jump around!

JUMP UP, JUMP UP AND GET DOWN!

↑ ↑ ↗ → ↘ ↓

JUMP! JUMP!

JUMP! JUMP!

(Everybody Jump)

↑ ↑ ↑ ↑

JUMP! JUMP!

JUMP! ↑ JUMP!

↑

SONG
Jump Around
ARTIST
House of Pain
YEAR
1992

SONGSPIRATION CONTEXT

Jumping was a big thing in 1992 hip-hop. In April that year, the teenage duo Kris Kross went to #1 in America with their song 'Jump', where they promise to make you jump. A group called *The Movement* reached #53 in August with the club-banger 'Jump!', where they implore, 'Jump everybody, jump everybody, jump' over and over. There was also 'White Men Can't Jump' by Riff, which reached #90 in May. 'Jump Around' came after all of these, peaking at #3 in October. (songfacts.com)

FEATURED FONTS

Each created in the year of the song release (from top to bottom, left to right)

Bodoni, International Mini Pics

Classified and available through identifont.com

Design: i_dbuero × Thomas Hofmann

Eis-
bär'n
müssen
nie
weinen

27

FEBRUARY

SONG
Eisbaer
ARTIST
Grauzone
YEAR
1980

SONGSPIRATION CONTEXT

Today is official Polar Bear Day. The band Grauzone sang in 1980: 'Polar bears never have to cry' – but now things look different. Not only is global warming killing off their population, brainless trophy hunters still shoot over 1,000 of them every year. There are only about 25,000 polar bears left in the world.

FEATURED FONTS

Each created in the year of the song release (from top to bottom, left to right)

Crillee

Classified and available through identifont.com

Design: i_dbuero × OA Krimmel

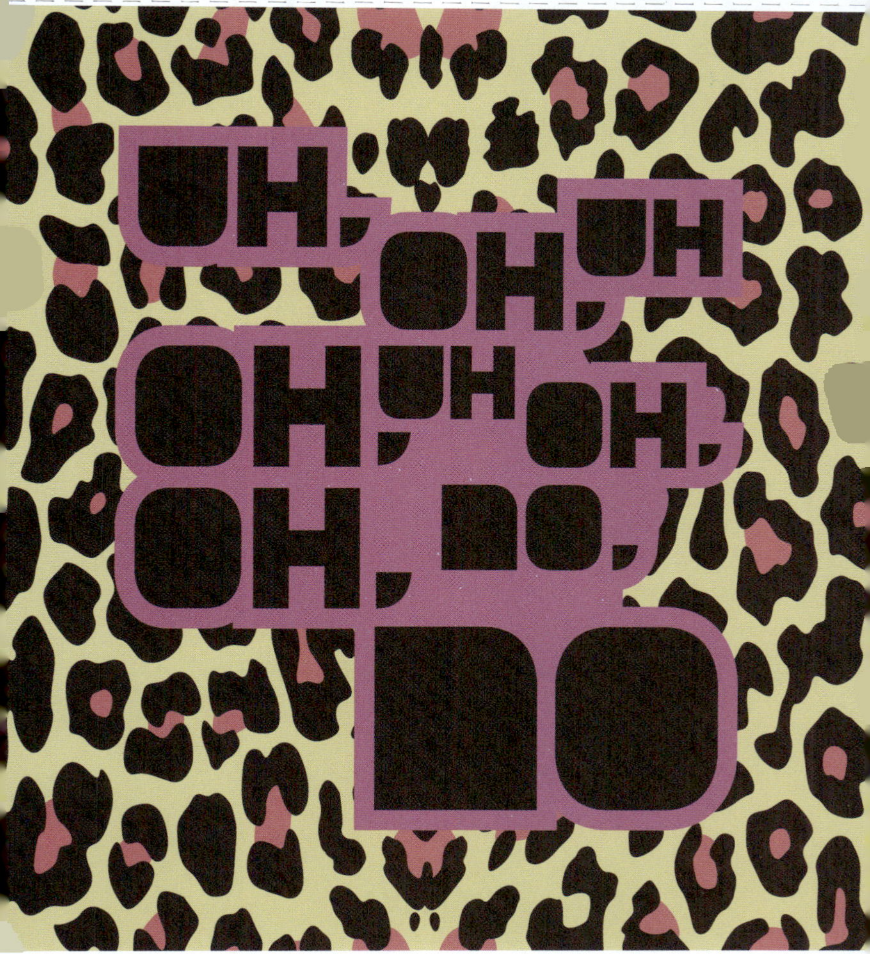

UH, OH, UH
OH, UH OH,
OH, NO,
NO

FEBRUARY

SONG
Crazy in Love
ARTIST
Beyoncé
YEAR
2003

SONGSPIRATION CONTEXT

There are crazy things you can do when you're 'crazy in love'. For example, thinking up a chorus like this and having your husband rap to it. The track record of this song is also very crazy: 600 million views on YouTube, 700 million streams on Spotify, many millions of singles and albums sold worldwide. And VH1 named it the 'Greatest Song of the '00s'. Crazy.

FEATURED FONTS

Each created in the year of the song release (from top to bottom, left to right)

BreakBeat Solid

Classified and available through identifont.com

Design: i_dbuero × OA Krimmel

IT'S OKAY

THIS IS A LEAP YEAR

FEBRUARY

SONG
Venus Kissed the Moon

ARTIST
Christine Lavin

YEAR
1990

SONGSPIRATION CONTEXT
A year is not a leap year if it's NOT divisible by 4,
OR if it's divisible by 100 AND NOT divisible by 400.
So 2024 is a leap year, 2025 isn't. Okay?

FEATURED FONTS
Each created in the year of the song release (from top to bottom, left to right)

Valet

Classified and available through identifont.com

Design: i_dbuero × OA Krimmel

MAKING EACH DAY A NEW CELEBRATION

SONG
Spring Vacation
ARTIST
The Beach Boys
YEAR
2012

SONGSPIRATION CONTEXT
Good vibrations: the Beach Boys are reunited after decades again. And life seem lighter and happier in spring. ‘Summer weather / We’re back together’.

FEATURED FONTS
Each created in the year of the song release (from top to bottom, left to right)

Kokoschka-Print

Classified and available through identifont.com

Design: i_dbuero × Evelyn Binder

THERE'S NO THING YOU CAN DO THAT CAN'T BE DONE

SONG
All You Need Is Love
ARTIST
The Beatles
YEAR
1967

SONGSPIRATION CONTEXT

On Monday, 2 March 1964, The Beatles began shooting their very first film, the as-yet untitled *A Hard Day's Night*. One of the actresses present on this day was Pattie Boyd, for whom George Harrison took an instant liking. They began dating shortly afterwards and got married ... *(to be continued tomorrow)*

FEATURED FONTS

Each created in the year of the song release (from top to bottom, left to right)

Classified and available through identifont.com

Design: i_dbuero × OA Krimmel

THERE'S
NO
THING
YOU CAN SING
THAT CAN'T
BE SUNG

SONG
All You Need Is Love
ARTIST
The Beatles
YEAR
1967

SONGSPIRATION CONTEXT
... Several years later Pattie Boyd left George Harrison due to his affair with Ringo Starr's wife Maureen, to get married to Harrison's friend Eric Clapton. Quite a lot of drama, worthy of a film.

FEATURED FONTS
Each created in the year of the song release (from top to bottom, left to right)

Classified and available through identifont.com

Design: i_dbuero × OA Krimmel

Don't stop thinking about tomorrow

4

MARCH

SONG
Don't Stop
ARTIST
Fleetwood Mac
YEAR
1977

SONGSPIRATION CONTEXT

On this day in 1918, the Spanish flu first appeared – in an American military hospital (although there are many other theories, this is the most likely). Within hours, hundreds of soldiers fell ill, and over the next months and years, half the world did too. It is estimated that over 50 million people died from it.

FEATURED FONTS

Each created in the year of the song release (from top to bottom, left to right)

Chesterfield

Classified and available through identifont.com

Design: i_dbuero × Carsten Güth

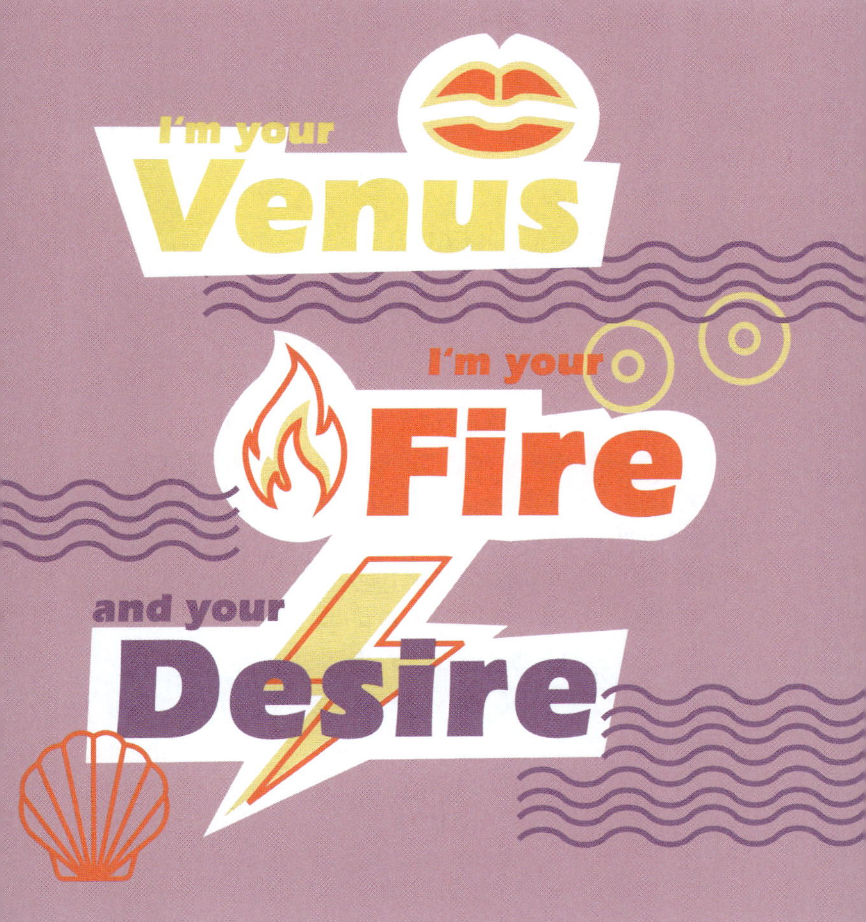
I'm your
Venus
I'm your
Fire
and your
Desire

SONG
Venus
ARTIST
Bananarama
YEAR
1986

SONGSPIRATION CONTEXT

Venera 14 landed on Venus on 5 March 1982. The Russian spacecraft was not the first, by the way. To date, 42 (we wink at Douglas Adams) space missions have flown to Venus. Initiated by the Americans, the Russians, the Europeans and the Japanese. Venus is very attractive – for bands as well as for governments.

FEATURED FONTS

Each created in the year of the song release (from top to bottom, left to right)

ITC Eras

Classified and available through identifont.com

Design: i_dbuero × Evelyn Binder

ES KÖNNT'

4lles

SO EINFACH SEIN, IST ES ABER NICHT.

SONG
Einfach sein
ARTIST
Die Fantastischen Vier
YEAR
2007

SONGSPIRATION CONTEXT

Today is Smudo's birthday (born in 1968). Smudo once spoke about how he had warbled the refrain "It could all be so simple, but it's not" on a trial basis in the studio: "And everyone thought it sounded somehow like Herbert [Grönemeyer]. So we thought: we could give him a call. We told him: 'Herbert, we have a number that sounds a bit like you. Would you be interested?' And he was – sometimes it can be so 'simple'.

FEATURED FONTS

Each created in the year of the song release (from top to bottom, left to right)

Aaux ProUltra

Classified and available through identifont.com

Design: i_dbuero × Sabine Schneider

BAKER
MAN IS
BAKING
BREAD

SONG
Bakerman
ARTIST
Laid Back
YEAR
1989

SONGSPIRATION CONTEXT

None other than Lars von Trier shot the music video for this catchy tune. In the humorous video, the Danish band jumps out of a plane as a parachute troop, sings the song and plays their instruments. The cryptic expression *'Sagabona kunjani wena'* in the song means 'Hello, how are you?' and comes from African Swahili. 'Bakerman is baking bread. The night train is coming. Sagabona kunjani wena?' Lyrics really can't be more 'laid back'.

FEATURED FONTS

Each created in the year of the song release (from top to bottom, left to right)

Manito

Classified and available through identifont.com

Design: i_dbuero × Syl Hillier

You make me feel like a natural woman

SONG
(You Make Me Feel) Natural Woman
ARTIST
Aretha Franklin
YEAR
1968

SONGSPIRATION CONTEXT

Today is International Women's Day.
"American history wells up when Aretha sings, nobody embodies more fully the connection between the African-American spiritual, the blues, R&B, rock and roll – the way that hardship and sorrow were transformed into something full of beauty and vitality and hope." (Barack Obama about Aretha Franklin)

FEATURED FONTS

Each created in the year of the song release (from top to bottom, left to right)
Forma DJR

Classified and available through identifont.com

Design: i_dbuero × Carsten Güth

I'm too young to fall asleep

SONG
Head Above Water
ARTIST
Avril Lavigne
YEAR
2018

SONGSPIRATION CONTEXT

'Head above Water' is about Lavigne's battle with Lyme disease, which can cause fatigue and joint pain, and is potentially fatal. She had faded from the public spotlight for a while because she was fighting off the disease. In bed and on the couch, she turned to writing music to get her through the situation. "Those were the worst years of my life as I went through both physical and emotional battles," the singer wrote. "I was able to turn that fight into music I'm really proud of." (songfacts.com)

FEATURED FONTS

Each created in the year of the song release (from top to bottom, left to right)

Standard

Classified and available through identifont.com

Design: i_dbuero × Evelyn Binder

MARCH

SONG

Istanbul (not Constantinople)

ARTIST

They Might Be Giants

YEAR

1953/1990

SONGSPIRATION CONTEXT

In 1626, the legendary sale of the island, now called Manhattan, by the Algonquin Indians took place. In their language, 'Manna-hatta' probably meant hilly island, but it can also mean place of intoxication, depending on the pronunciation. For goods worth 60 guilders at the time, Peter Minuit, as deputy of the Dutch king in America, received the island.

FEATURED FONTS

Each created in the year of the song release (from top to bottom, left to right)

Glitzy Regular, Glitzy Curl, Glitzy Jewel

Classified and available through identifont.com

Design: i_dbuero × OA Krimmel

stuck in a maze
Everything's
okay
but it's
not really ok

SONG
Maze
ARTIST
Juice WRLD
YEAR
2019

SONGSPIRATION CONTEXT

The World Health Organization declared officially on this day in 2020 that the COVID-19 outbreak was a pandemic.

FEATURED FONTS

Each created in the year of the song release (from top to bottom, left to right)

Modern Love Grunge, Obviously

Classified and available through identifont.com

Design: i_dbuero × Evelyn Binder

But I
would walk

500 miles

And I
would walk

500 more

SONG
I'm Gonna Be (500 Miles)

ARTIST
The Proclaimers

YEAR
1987

SONGSPIRATION CONTEXT

On 12 March (1930), Mahatma Gandhi began his spectacular salt march against the then British salt monopoly. The march was 385 kilometres long and took him to the Arabian Sea, where he symbolically collected grains of salt. His non-violent resistance ultimately led to independence for India.

FEATURED FONTS

Each created in the year of the song release (from top to bottom, left to right)

Retail Script, Pragmatica

Classified and available through identifont.com

Design: i_dbuero × Carsten Güth

THE TIME IS

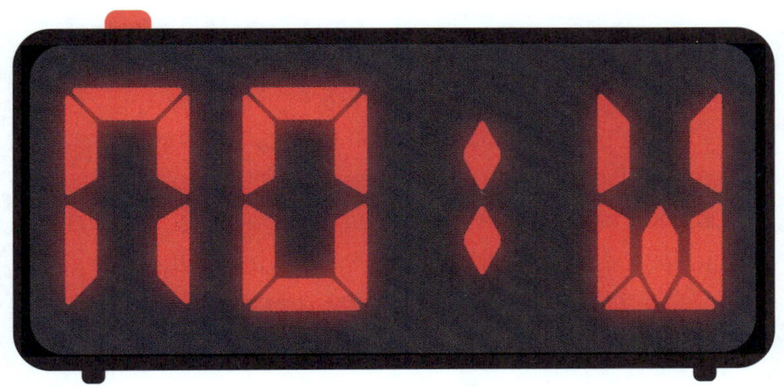

SONG
The Time Is Now
ARTIST
Moloko
YEAR
2000

SONGSPIRATION CONTEXT

Róisín Murphy and Mark Brydon met at a party in Sheffield, where Murphy asked Brydon "Do you like my tight sweater?", which would later become the title of Moloko's debut album. After that party, the two became a couple, both musically and privately.

FEATURED FONTS

Each created in the year of the song release (from top to bottom, left to right)

DIN, Calculus LCD

Classified and available through identifont.com

Design: i_dbuero × Carsten Güth

Because
the night
belongs
to
Lovers

SONG
Because the Night
ARTIST
Patti Smith
YEAR
1978

SONGSPIRATION CONTEXT

White Day (March 14): In South Korea and Japan, couples celebrate two 'Valentine's Days'. On February 14th, women give chocolate to men and the following month on 'White Day' men reciprocate by giving non-chocolate candy.

FEATURED FONTS

Each created in the year of the song release (from top to bottom, left to right)

Balmoral, ITC Clearface

Classified and available through identifont.com

Design: i_dbuero × Carsten Güth

OOGA
CHAKA
OOGA
OOGA

MARCH

SONG
Hooked on a Feeling

ARTIST
Blue Swede (Original: B.J. Thomas)

YEAR
1974 (Original 1968)

SONGSPIRATION CONTEXT

In 1971, British musician Jonathan King recorded a cover version of this song, for the first time adding the meaningless 'ooga chaka' jungle chants. Later also Blue Swede and others used that famous intro for their hit cover. And now everybody:

Ooga-Chaka Ooga-Ooga
Ooga-Chaka Ooga-Ooga
Ooga-Chaka Ooga-Ooga
Ooga-Chaka Ooga-Ooga.

FEATURED FONTS

Each created in the year of the song release (from top to bottom, left to right)

Helvetica Ultra Condensed

Classified and available through identifont.com

Design: i_dbuero × Martin Drozmann

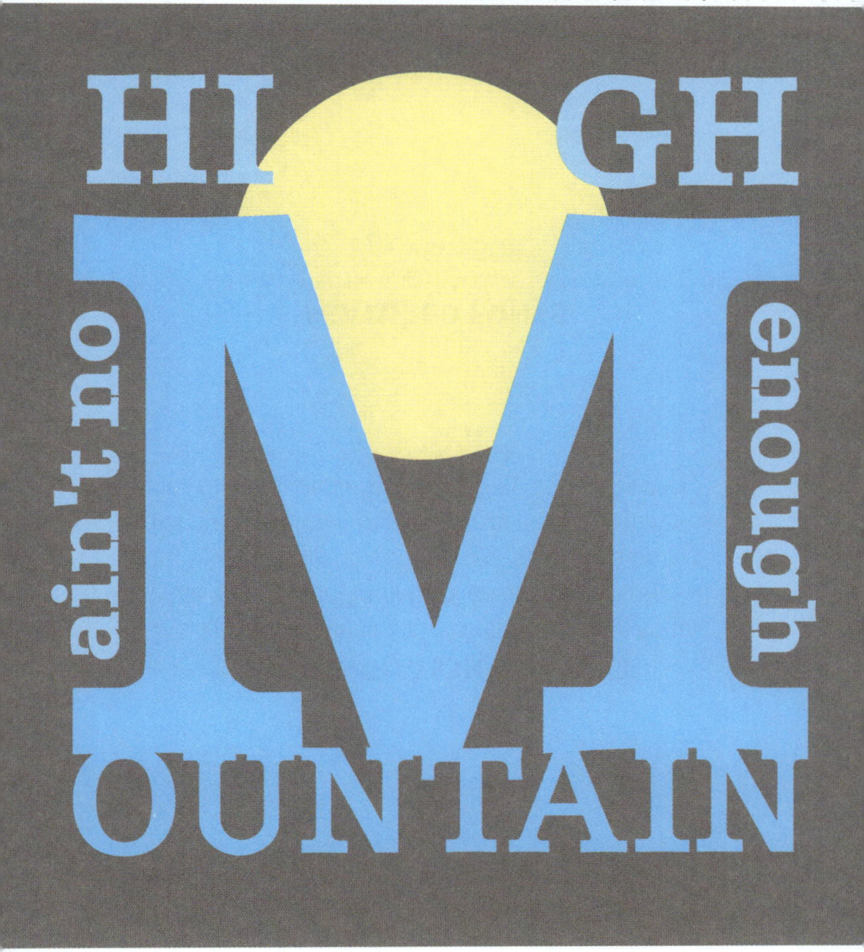

HIGH

ain't no

enough

MOUNTAIN

MARCH

SONG
Ain't No Mountain High Enough
ARTIST
Marvin Gaye & Tammi Terrell
YEAR
1967

SONGSPIRATION CONTEXT

Motown stars Tammi and Marvin were not a couple, but friends for life. Until Tammi collapsed into his arms at a concert. Shortly thereafter, she was diagnosed with a brain tumour – this mountain then tragically became too high for her. Tammi died on March 16, 1970; she was only 24 years old.

FEATURED FONTS

Each created in the year of the song release (from top to bottom, left to right)

Egyptian 505

Classified and available through identifont.com

Design: i_dbuero × OA Krimmel

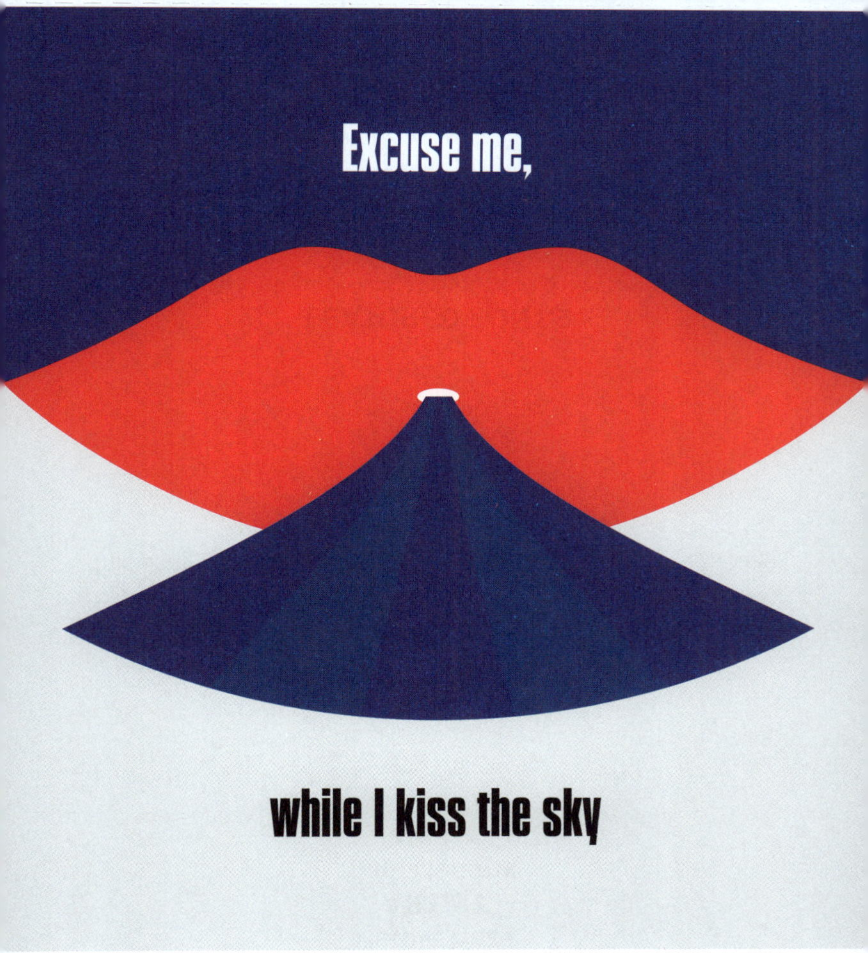

Excuse me,

while I kiss the sky

SONG
Purple Haze
ARTIST
Jimi Hendrix
YEAR
1967

SONGSPIRATION CONTEXT

On March 17 1967 the second single by The Jimi Hendrix Experience was released. Because of ambiguities in the lyrics, this song seems to refer to a psychedelic experience, although Jimi described it as a love song ;-)

FEATURED FONTS

Each created in the year of the song release (from top to bottom, left to right)

Press Gothic

Classified and available through identifont.com

Design: i_dbuero × Carsten Güth

18

MARCH

SONG
Oh Yeah
ARTIST
Yello
YEAR
1997

SONGSPIRATION CONTEXT

"I was not inspired by this song [tunes], I didn't like it at all, but then Boris [Blank] told me a story and said 'You imagine you're the King of Tonga ... some people bring you the perfect drink, a cool breeze comes to you. In this situation what would you say?' And I said, 'Oh Yeah!'" (Dieter Meier)

FEATURED FONTS

Each created in the year of the song release (from top to bottom, left to right)

Magistral

Classified and available through identifont.com

Design: i_dbuero × OA Krimmel

I'll be your

Substitute

SONG
Substitute
ARTIST
Clout
YEAR
1978 (1975)

SONGSPIRATION CONTEXT

The disco diva Gloria Gaynor covered this song in 1978 at the insistence of her record company. At the same session she also recorded a song called 'I Will Survive', which was only released as a B side to her single 'Substitute'. This single only made it to #107, but most DJs flipped it and played the B side, so it was soon re-released with the sides flipped and 'I Will Survive' shot to #1.

FEATURED FONTS

Each created in the year of the song release (from top to bottom, left to right)

Leamington

Classified and available through identifont.com

Design: i_dbuero × Evelyn Binder

In every

life

we have some

trouble

but when you

worry

you make it

double

20

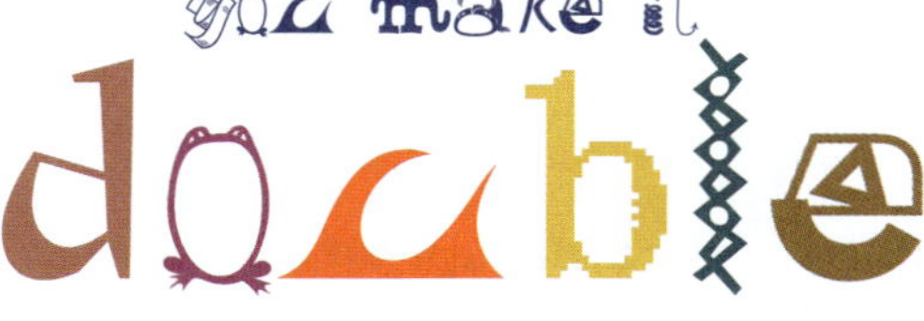

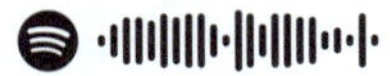

MARCH

SONG
Don't Worry, Be Happy

ARTIST
Bobby McFerrin

YEAR
1988

SONGSPIRATION CONTEXT

Today is World Happiness Day!
By the way, 'Don't Worry, Be Happy' is a quote from the Indian guru Meher Baba. He was fed up with the bad vibe of people and kept silent from 10 July 1925 onwards for the remaining 44 years of his life. A rather special way to become happier. Not recommended for imitation, singing seems to do the trick.

FEATURED FONTS

Each created in the year of the song release (from top to bottom, left to right)

Old Dreadful No.7 BT

Classified and available through identifont.com

Design: i_dbuero × Sabine Schneider

Daylight come and I'm wan' go home

SONG
Banana Boat Song (Day-O)

ARTIST
Harry Belafonte

YEAR
1956

SONGSPIRATION CONTEXT

Six artists hit the US Top 40 with 'The Banana Boat Song' in 1957: The Terriers' version was the first to chart at #4 (#15 in the UK), followed by Belafonte, The Fontane Sisters (#13), Steve Lawrence (#18), Sarah Vaughan (#19), and Stan Freberg, whose comedy version hit #25. Today Harry Belafonte's version is the most famous – and today is his birthday (born in 1927).

FEATURED FONTS

Each created in the year of the song release (from top to bottom, left to right)

Helvetica Neue

Classified and available through identifont.com

Design: i_dbuero × Evelyn Binder

DON'T GO
CHASING

WATERFALLS

22

MARCH

SONG
Waterfalls
ARTIST
TLC
YEAR
1995

SONGSPIRATION CONTEXT

Today is World Water Day.
We really have every reason to celebrate and dance to this song, for example. Because in the entire universe, not a single permanent presence of liquid water has been detected – except on our good old Mother Earth. To your health!

FEATURED FONTS

Each created in the year of the song release (from top to bottom, left to right)

Haettenschweiler

Classified and available through identifont.com

Design: i_dbuero × Hannah Hoffmann

IN THIS GREAT FUTURE YOU CAN'T FORGET YOUR PAST

MARCH

SONG
No Woman No Cry

ARTIST
Bob Marley & The Wailers

YEAR
1974

SONGSPIRATION CONTEXT

This famous song has taken on many different meanings in the years since it was written and performed, but as Bob Marley himself commented, when he spoke, sang or put forward his thoughts, they were simple. This song is about his life growing up in the housing project in Trenchtown and his relationship with his mother. 'No woman, nuh cry' means 'no woman, don't cry'. 'Nuh' means don't.

FEATURED FONTS

Each created in the year of the song release (from top to bottom, left to right)

ITC Lubalin Graph

Classified and available through identifont.com

Design: i_dbuero × Tim Oliver Schweizer

SOME-
TIMES
YOU
STAND
SOME-
TIMES
YOU
BEND

SONG
Life is a Highway
ARTIST
Rascal Flatts
YEAR
2008

SONGSPIRATION CONTEXT

Ask any of the members of Rascal Flatts what their name actually means, and they wouldn't be able to give you an answer. They realized they didn't have a name as they were getting ready to sign with Lyric Street Records. A friend had a band in the 60s named Rascal Flatts and suggested it, and the rest is history!

FEATURED FONTS

Each created in the year of the song release (from top to bottom, left to right)

Lekton

Classified and available through identifont.com

Design: i_dbuero × Evelyn Binder

HOLD ME CLOSER TINY DANCER

SONG
Tiny Dancer
ARTIST
Elton John
YEAR
1971

SONGSPIRATION CONTEXT

"Music has healing power. It has the ability to take people out of themselves for a few hours."
(Elton John)
On this day, Sir Elton John was born in 1947.

FEATURED FONTS

Each created in the year of the song release (from top to bottom, left to right)

Jackson MN

Classified and available through identifont.com

Design: i_dbuero × Sabine Schneider

I'D ——— RATHER

WITH THE

THAN CRY

WITH THE

SONG
Only the Good Die Young
ARTIST
Billy Joel
YEAR
1977

SONGSPIRATION RELATION

Raymond Chandler was an American author and is considered one of the pioneers of the American hardboiled novels. He died on 26 March 1959. For his crime novels, Chandler invented the character of the melancholy private detective Philip Marlowe (played in films by Humphrey Bogart and Robert Mitchum, among others).

FEATURED FONTS

Each created in the year of the song release (from top to bottom, left to right)

Garamond Book, Benguiat Pro ITC, ITC Fenice Std

Classified and available through identifont.com

Design: i_dbuero × Hanna Spitznagel

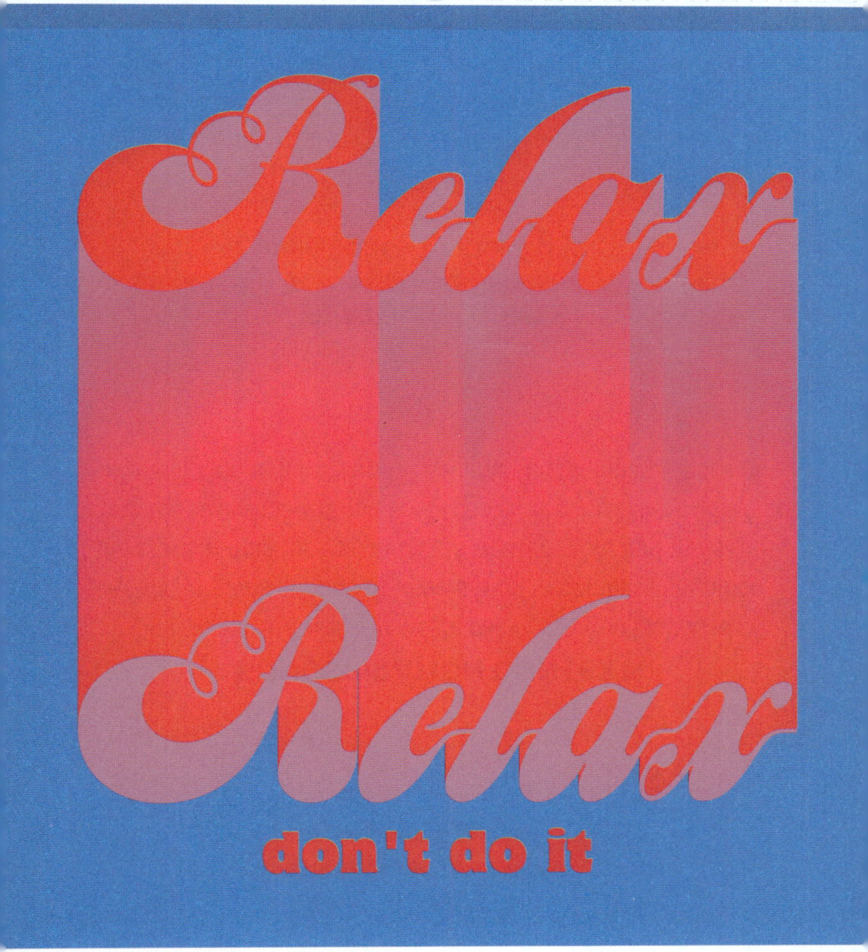

Relax

Relax

don't do it

MARCH

SONG
Relax
ARTIST
Frankie Goes to Hollywood
YEAR
1983

SONGSPIRATION CONTEXT

On this day in 1998, the magic pill Viagra was launched. Actually, it was supposed to be a drug to combat high blood pressure, but as the test subjects wanted more and more of it during the test phase, it quickly became clear that there was more potential hidden here – and it became the famous potency pill.

FEATURED FONTS

Each created in the year of the song release (from top to bottom, left to right)

Julia Script, Motter Corpus

Classified and available through identifont.com

Design: i_dbuero × Carsten Güth

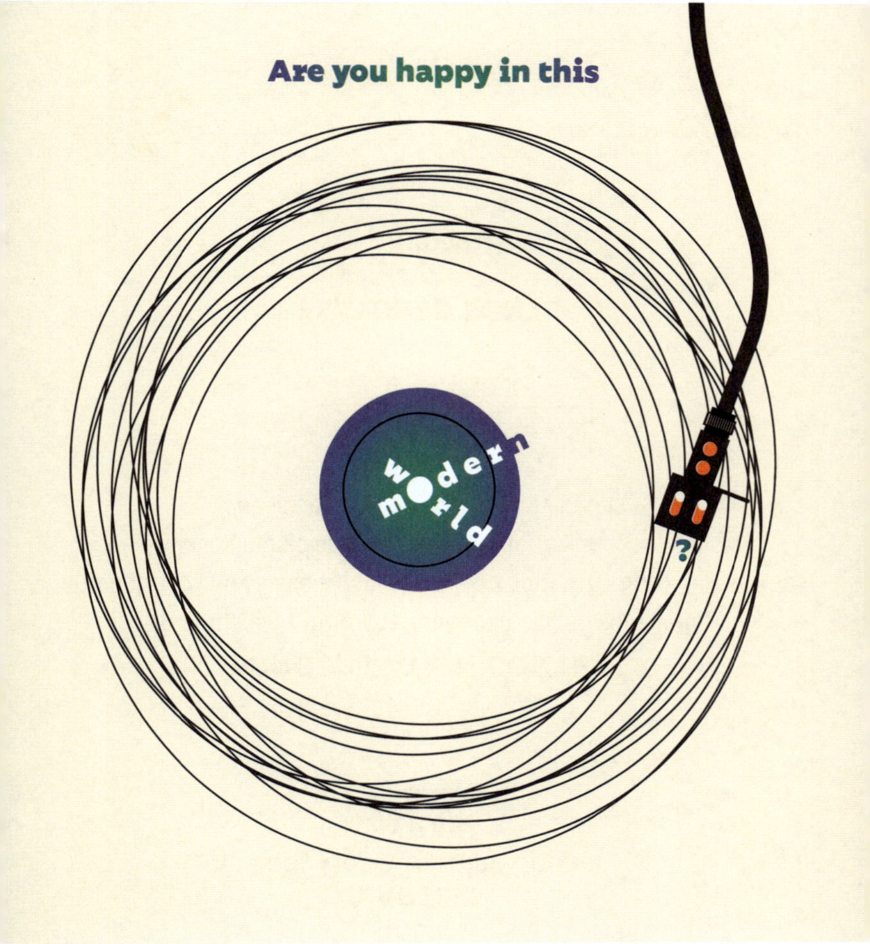

Are you happy in this

MARCH

SONG
Shallow
ARTIST
Lady Gaga, Bradley Cooper
YEAR
2018

SONGSPIRATION CONTEXT

On this day in 1986, the American singer, songwriter and actress Lady Gaga was born in New York City. She's one of the best-selling music artists in this modern world, so one can guess she can be quite happy in this.

FEATURED FONTS

Each created in the year of the song release (from top to bottom, left to right)

Bilbao

Classified and available through identifont.com

Design: i_dbuero × OA Krimmel

and so you're **back**

from OUTER SPACE

SONG
I Will Survive
ARTIST
Gloria Gaynor
YEAR
1978

SONGSPIRATION CONTEXT
'I Will Survive' has become a symbol of female empowerment, and in 2016 the original recording was recognized as "culturally, historically, or artistically significant" enough to be preserved in the 'National Library of Congress' National Recording Registry.

FEATURED FONTS
Each created in the year of the song release (from top to bottom, left to right)

ITC Zapf Dingbats, URW Helserif

Classified and available through identifont.com

Design: i_dbuero × Evelyn Binder

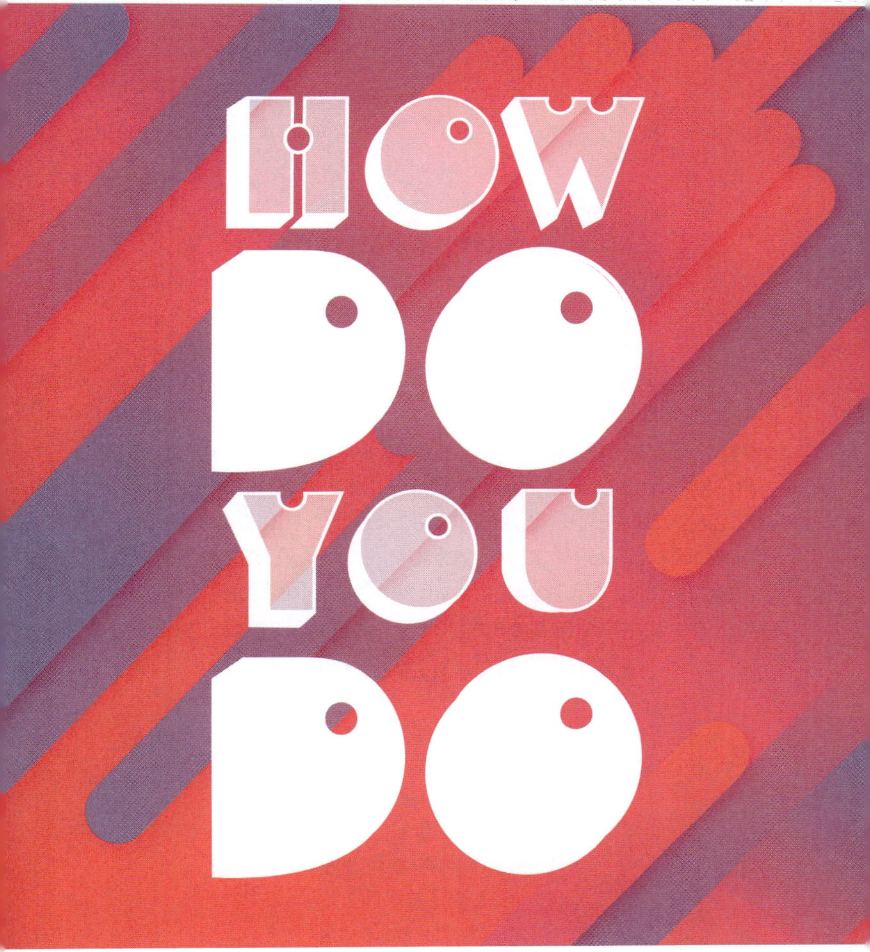

HOW DO YOU DO

MARCH

SONG
How Do You Do
ARTIST
Mouth & MacNeal
YEAR
1972

SONGSPIRATION CONTEXT

If the testimonies from the two artists are to be believed, it was antipathy at first sight. Before the collaboration, neither had any success: Mouth (Willem Duyn) said laconically in an interview: "Two flops together. At the beginning I didn't believe in it that much. I thought it would go wrong again."
But the duo worked together and outwardly they appeared harmonious, but at the end of 1974 the record contract came to an end and the two never saw each other again.

FEATURED FONTS

Each created in the year of the song release (from top to bottom, left to right)

Shotgun Blanks

Classified and available through identifont.com

Design: i_dbuero × Evelyn Binder

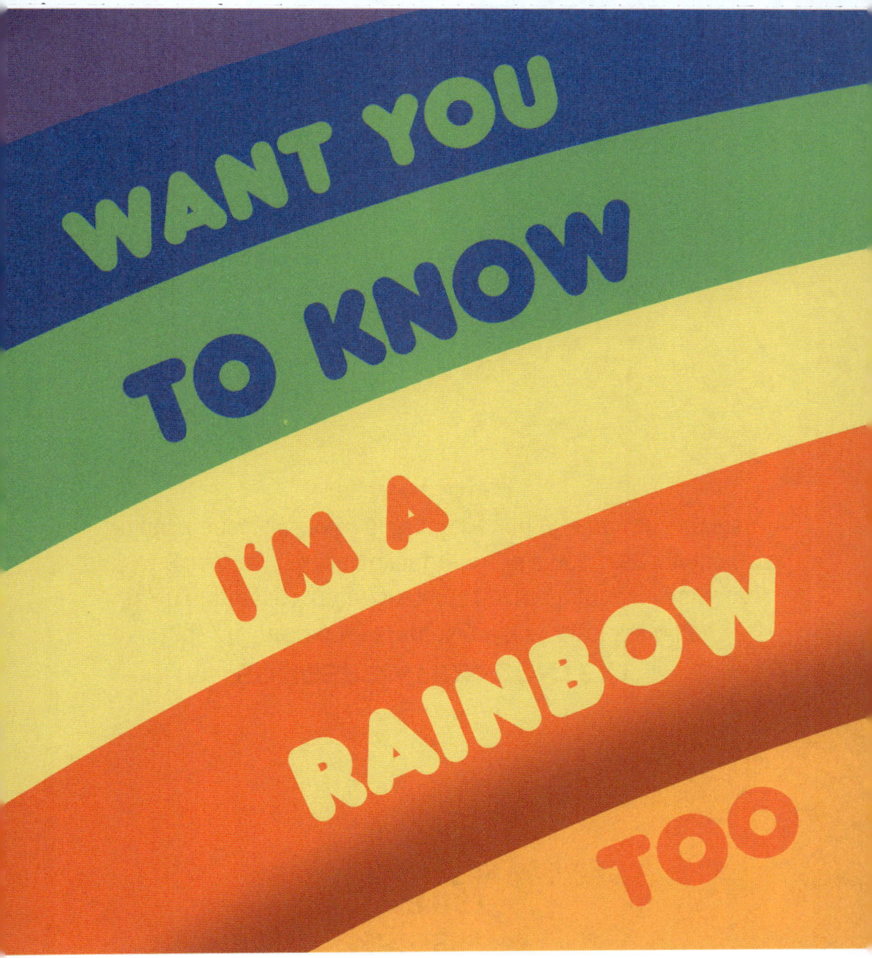

WANT YOU
TO KNOW
I'M A
RAINBOW
TOO

MARCH

SONG
Sun Is Shining

ARTIST
Bob Marley & The Wailers

YEAR
1978

SONGSPIRATION CONTEXT
Today is International Transgender Day of Visibility. As an impressive natural spectacle, the rainbow has been part of religious myths all over the world since time immemorial. In most cases, it takes on the function of a bridge between heaven and earth.

FEATURED FONTS
Each created in the year of the song release (from top to bottom, left to right)

Frankfurter EF Solid

Classified and available through identifont.com

Design: i_dbuero × Sabine Schneider

SONG
Fool's Day
ARTIST
Lloyd Clarke
YEAR
1962

SONGSPIRATION CONTEXT

April Fools!

FEATURED FONTS

Each created in the year of the song release (from top to bottom, left to right)

Invisible Extended, No Complain Bold

Classified and available through identifont.com

Design: i_dbuero × OA Krimmel

The answer
MY FRIEND
is blowin'
in the
wind

SONG
Blowin' in the Wind
ARTIST
Bob Dylan
YEAR
1963

SONGSPIRATION CONTEXT

"There ain't too much I can say about this song except that the answer is blowing in the wind. It ain't in no book or movie or TV show or discussion group. Man, it's in the wind – and it's blowing in the wind. Too many of these hip people are telling me where the answer is but oh I won't believe that [...]"
(Bob Dylan, 1963 in an interview)

FEATURED FONTS

Each created in the year of the song release (from top to bottom, left to right)

Roberta

Classified and available through identifont.com

Design: i_dbuero × Sabine Schneider

Winter, spring, summer or fall
All you have to do is ...
... call

SONG
You've Got a Friend
ARTIST
Carole King
YEAR
1971

SONGSPIRATION CONTEXT

On April 3, 1973, a Motorola researcher made the first ever mobile telephone call from handheld subscriber equipment, placing a call to his rival at Bell Labs. Since then, a lot has changed on our mobile devices. But you can still call someone at least ...

FEATURED FONTS

Each created in the year of the song release (from top to bottom, left to right)

Classified and available through identifont.com

Design: i_dbuero × Carsten Güth

WHAT A DIFFERENCE A DAY MAKES

SONG
What a Difference a Day Makes
ARTIST
Esther Phillips (Original Dinah Washington)
YEAR
1975 (1959)

SONGSPIRATION CONTEXT

The number of cover versions is a good indicator of how great a song is. Or that, as in this case, 25 years later such a version storms back into the charts. Dinah Washington's original version has been in the Grammy Hall of Fame since 1998. The disco version by Esther Phillips has also become an evergreen. And the message is always the same, a catchy phrase to which the SONG-SPIRATION team totally agrees: *What a Difference a Day Makes*!

FEATURED FONTS

Each created in the year of the song release (from top to bottom, left to right)

Pump Triline, Buxom

Classified and available through identifont.com

Design: i_dbuero × Carsten Güth

I read the **NEWS** today,

Oh boy...

SONG
A Day in the Life
ARTIST
The Beatles
YEAR
1967

SONGSPIRATION CONTEXT

"Paul and I were definitely working together, especially on 'A Day in the Life' ... The way we wrote a lot of the time: you'd write the good bit, the part that was easy, like "I read the news today" or whatever it was, then when you got stuck or whenever it got hard, instead of carrying on, you just drop it; then we would meet each other, and I would sing half, and he would be inspired to write the next bit and vice versa."
(John Lennon)

FEATURED FONTS

Each created in the year of the song release (from top to bottom, left to right)

Concorde, Press Gothic, Ecsetiras

Classified and available through identifont.com

Design: i_dbuero × OA Krimmel

I've been looking so long at these pictures of you

SONG
Pictures of You
ARTIST
The Cure
YEAR
1990

SONGSPIRATION CONTEXT

This song was exceptionally used in a Hewlett-Packard commercial. Robert Smith: “I’m so against music in adverts, it f--king killed me even agreeing to that, but it was the only way. The money generated from those adverts went into buying me control on our back catalogue, otherwise it would have been like mortgaging the band.”

FEATURED FONTS

Each created in the year of the song release (from top to bottom, left to right)

Newberlin

Classified and available through identifont.com

Design: i_dbuero × Carsten Güth

Isn‘t it
strange

SONG
Strange
ARTIST
Celeste
YEAR
2019

SONGSPIRATION CONTEXT

Isn't it strange
How people can change
From strangers to friends
Friends into lovers
And strangers again?
(Celeste)

FEATURED FONTS

Each created in the year of the song release (from top to bottom, left to right)

TT Trailors, Standard 100

Classified and available through
identifont.com

Design: i_dbuero × Carsten Güth

Oh,

SINNER MAN

where you gonna run to ?

SONG
Sinnerman
ARTIST
Nina Simone
YEAR
1962

SONGSPIRATION CONTEXT

"Some of my most fantastic experiences – experiences that really shake me, now that I think of them – happened in the church when we'd have these revival meetings.
I'd be playiNnNnNnNnNng, boy! I'd really be playing. I loved it!
Folks would be shoutin' all over the place.
Now that's my background!"
(Nina Simone in *Ebony*, 1969)

FEATURED FONTS

Each created in the year of the song release (from top to bottom, left to right)

Lazurski, Square 721

Classified and available through identifont.com

Design: i_dbuero × Evelyn Binder

space ain't man's final frontier

man's final frontier is the soul

SONG
Man's Final Frontier
ARTIST
Arrested Development
YEAR
1992

SONGSPIRATION CONTEXT

On April 9, 1959, the National Aeronautics and Space Administration (NASA) introduces America's first astronauts to the press: Scott Carpenter, L. Gordon Cooper Jr., John H. Glenn Jr., Virgil 'Gus' Grissom, Walter Schirra Jr., Alan Shepard Jr. and Donald Slayton, dubbed as the 'Mercury Seven'.

FEATURED FONTS

Each created in the year of the song release (from top to bottom, left to right)

Elektron, Inform

Classified and available through identifont.com

Design: i_dbuero × Carsten Güth

So give me coffee and TV, peacefully

SONG
Coffee & TV
ARTIST
Blur
YEAR
1999

SONGSPIRATION CONTEXT

"Behind every successful British band
is a substantial amount of coffee and TV."
(oak)

FEATURED FONTS

Each created in the year of the song release (from top to bottom, left to right)

Son Gothic

Classified and available through
identifont.com

Design: i_dbuero × Carsten Güth

Now is not the time to cry

SONG
Live Forever

ARTIST
Oasis

YEAR
1994

SONGSPIRATION CONTEXT

On this day in 1814 Napoleon Bonaparte abdicates unconditionally and is exiled to the island of Elba in the Mediterranean.

FEATURED FONTS

Each created in the year of the song release (from top to bottom, left to right)

FF Dirty One

Classified and available through identifont.com

Design: i_dbuero × Carsten Güth

MONEY

IT'S A

SOUL

12

APRIL

SONG
Money
ARTIST
Pink Floyd
YEAR
1973

SONGSPIRATION CONTEXT

Actually, the lyrics were a critique of the power of money and how it changes people's character for the worse, with lines such as "I'm in the high-fidelity first-class travelling set / And I think I need a Lear jet". In the end, however, the sales of the album *The Dark Side of the Moon*, from which this song is taken, would have been enough for several Lear jets for Led Zeppelin.

FEATURED FONTS

Each created in the year of the song release (from top to bottom, left to right)

Pierrot

Classified and available through identifont.com

Design: i_dbuero × Sabine Schneider

Money
for
nothing

SONG
Money for Nothing
ARTIST
Dire Straits
YEAR
1985

SONGSPIRATION CONTEXT

The idea for this song came to Mark Knopfler when he was in an electronics shop and noticed the salesman gazing in awe at the wall of televisions showing MTV everywhere. If you listen carefully, you will recognise Sting's voice in the line "I want my MTV". Sting was near the studio at the time of the recording – windsurfing.

FEATURED FONTS

Each created in the year of the song release (from top to bottom, left to right)

URW Grotesk

Classified and available through identifont.com

Design: i_dbuero × Carsten Güth

MONEY

14

APRIL

SONG
Money, Money, Money
ARTIST
ABBA
YEAR
1985

SONGSPIRATION CONTEXT

The baroque pop number by Agnetha, Björn, Benny and Anna-Frid brought the band exactly what they were singing about here: lots of money. For their comeback, the four were already offered 1 billion dollars in 2000. When their reunion finally came in 2021, there was possibly even more money on the table.

FEATURED FONTS

Each created in the year of the song release (from top to bottom, left to right)

LTFehrle Display

Classified and available through identifont.com

Design: i_dbuero × Evelyn Binder

PICTURE YOURSELF IN A BOAT ON A RIVER

APRIL

SONG
Lucy in the Sky with Diamonds
ARTIST
The Beatles
YEAR
1967

SONGSPIRATION CONTEXT

This song based on a surrealistic picture drawn by Julian Lennon, John's son, concerning his friend Lucy quite literally flying in a sky filled with diamonds. Its psychedelic images are trippy and also is the music ... Art inspires artists ... Today is World Art Day!

FEATURED FONTS

Each created in the year of the song release (from top to bottom, left to right)

Amelia

Classified and available through identifont.com

Design: i_dbuero × Carsten Güth

Be-bop-
a-Lula

SONG
Be-bop-a-Lula
ARTIST
Gene Vincent
YEAR
1956

SONGSPIRATION CONTEXT

Gene Vincent took part in the talent contest held by the radio station WCMS in 1955. With his cover version of Elvis Presley's 'Heartbreak Hotel', he immediately convinced the jury, made it to the final round and sang 'Be-Bop-A-Lula' there for the first time. He won and had a demo recording made that was sent to Capitol Records. He had written the song in the hospital after a motor-cycle accident, inspired by the comic strip *Little Lulu*.
The rest is history.

FEATURED FONTS

Each created in the year of the song release (from top to bottom, left to right)

Schneidler Maxim

Classified and available through identifont.com

Design: i_dbuero × OA Krimmel

A-wop-bop-a-loo-bop-a-lop-bam-boom

17

APRIL

SONG
Tutti-Frutti
ARTIST
Little Richard
YEAR
1955

SONGSPIRATION CONTEXT

Little Richard wrote this song when he was working as a dishwasher. "I couldn't talk back to my boss man. He would bring all these pots back for me to wash, and one day I said, I've got to do something to stop this man bringing back all these pots to me to wash, and I said, 'Awap bop a lup bop a wop bam boom, take 'em out!' and that's what I meant at the time. And so I wrote 'tutti Frutti' in the kitchen, I wrote 'Good Golly Miss Molly' in the kitchen, I wrote 'Long Tall Sally in that kitchen." (Little Richard)

FEATURED FONTS

Each created in the year of the song release (from top to bottom, left to right)

Choc

Classified and available through identifont.com

Design: i_dbuero × OA Krimmel

Ski-bi dibby dib yo da dub dub / Yo da dub dub

SONG
Scatman (ski-ba-bop-ba-dop-bop)

ARTIST
Scatman John

YEAR
1995

SONGSPIRATION CONTEXT
John Paul Larkin suffered as a child from a severe stutter, which led him to have an emotionally traumatic childhood. At age 12, he began to learn the piano and was introduced to the art of scat singing two years later. Both helped him to express himself and to overcome his handicaps.

FEATURED FONTS
Each created in the year of the song release (from top to bottom, left to right)

Magneto

Classified and available through identifont.com

Design: i_dbuero × OA Krimmel

So let's do it like they do on the Discovery Channel

19

APRIL

SONG
The Bad Touch
ARTIST
Bloodhound Gang
YEAR
1999

SONGSPIRATION CONTEXT

Bloodhound Gang was notorious for their unconventional performances. Part of the show included Jimmy Pop throwing up on stage after sticking a banana down his throat or bassist Evil Jared Hasselhoff urinating on his head. They liked to eat worms, live insects and other animals on stage or during an interview. Actually also quite similar to what they do on the Discovery Channel.

FEATURED FONTS

Each created in the year of the song release (from top to bottom, left to right)

ABS 3

Classified and available through identifont.com

Design: i_dbuero × Evelyn Binder

LIVING
YOUNG
AND
WILD
AND
FREE

SONG
Young, Wild & Free
ARTIST
Snoop Dogg, Wiz Khalifa, Bruno Mars
YEAR
2011

SONGSPIRATION CONTEXT

Yep, that's right, there's actually that too: Today is Weed Day! Why exactly on 4/20?There are numerous unconfirmed myths about that. What is certain, however, is that today at 4:20 pm the most cannabis-infused vapor will rise worldwide. Snoop Dogg is certainly smoking his own marijuana there, Leafs by Snoop is the name of his successful start-up.

FEATURED FONTS

Each created in the year of the song release (from top to bottom, left to right)

Glob Glob

Classified and available through identifont.com

Design: i_dbuero × OA Krimmel

So tonight
I'M GONNA
party
LIKE IT'S
1999

SONG
1999
ARTIST
Prince
YEAR
1982

SONGSPIRATION CONTEXT

This song reached the Top 40 three times in three different decades – first in 1982, then in 1999 and again after Prince's passing on April 21, 2016. To be continued ...

FEATURED FONTS

Each created in the year of the song release (from top to bottom, left to right)

Challenge, Shannon, Van Dijk

Classified and available through identifont.com

Design: i_dbuero × Carsten Güth

We'll make
Heaven
a place on
Earth

SONG
Heaven is a Place on Earth
ARTIST
Belinda Carlisle
YEAR
1987

SONGSPIRATION CONTEXT

All your antennae out, it's Earth Day.
When Belinda Carlisle released this song in the late 80s, it climbed to number one everywhere, in Europe, in the USA, even in Zimbabwe. A beautiful mantra that we should all try to live by every day. Because there is no Planet B.

FEATURED FONTS

Each created in the year of the song release (from top to bottom, left to right)

Pragmatica, Bordeaux Script

Classified and available through identifont.com

Design: i_dbuero × Carsten Güth

who could ask for MO-O-O-O-O-ORE

SONG
1984
ARTIST
David Bowie
YEAR
1974

SONGSPIRATION CONTEXT

Most of David Bowie's *Diamond Dogs* tracks began life as songs for his planned cinema version of George Orwell's iconic novel *Nineteen Eighty-Four* – until the author's estate refused the rights. The most obvious remaining evidence is the eponymous track, a disco-noir thriller with lyrics about how Big Brother will "split your pretty cranium and fill it full of air". So let's celebrate International Book Day even more ethusiastically today!

FEATURED FONTS

Each created in the year of the song release (from top to bottom, left to right)

Baby Cakes NF

Classified and available through identifont.com

Design: i_dbuero × Sabine Schneider

all of us
get lost in the
darkness
DREAMERS
learn to steer by
the
stars

SONG
The Pass
ARTIST
Rush
YEAR
1989

SONGSPIRATION CONTEXT

The *Hubble Space Telescope* is launched by the Space Shuttle *Discovery* on 24 April 1990. The space telescope had a resolution that had never been achieved before. Its successor, the *James Webb Space Telescope*, launched in 2021. Unimaginably distant galaxies have since been made visible to us as photographs.

FEATURED FONTS

Each created in the year of the song release (from top to bottom, left to right)

Bodoni 72

Classified and available through identifont.com

Design: i_dbuero × Sabine Schneider

WHERE IS THE LIFE THAT I RECOGNIZE?

APRIL

SONG
Ordinary World
ARTIST
Duran Duran
YEAR
1993

SONGSPIRATION CONTEXT

"I'm not a snob. Ask anybody. Well, anybody who matters."
(Lead singer Simon Le Bon)

FEATURED FONTS

Each created in the year of the song release (from top to bottom, left to right)
Mythos

Classified and available through
identifont.com

Design: i_dbuero × Evelyn Binder

HELLO
DARKNESS,
MY
OLD
FRIEND...

SONG
The Sound of Silence

ARTIST
Simon & Garfunkel

YEAR
1964

SONGSPIRATION CONTEXT

21-year-old Paul Simon loved to write his lyrics in the bathroom with his guitar – because of the acoustics. And to be able to concentrate better, he turned off the light. Paul says "I've always believed that you need a truthful first line to kick you off into a song. You have to say something emotionally true before you can let your imagination wander."

FEATURED FONTS

Each created in the year of the song release (from top to bottom, left to right)

Miedinger

Classified and available through identifont.com

Design: i_dbuero × Evelyn Binder

HEY HO LET'S GO!

SONG
Blitzkrieg Bop
ARTIST
The Ramones
YEAR
1976

SONGSPIRATION CONTEXT

Joey Ramone explained: "I hate to blow the mystique, but at the time we really liked bubblegum music, and we really liked the Bay City Rollers. Their song 'Saturday Night' had a great chant in it, so we wanted a song with a chant in it: 'Hey! Ho! Let's Go!'. 'Blitzkrieg Bop' was our 'Saturday Night'." (songfacts.com)

FEATURED FONTS

Each created in the year of the song release (from top to bottom, left to right)

Frutiger

Classified and available through identifont.com

Design: i_dbuero × Sabine Schneider

VIVA LA VIDA

APRIL

SONG
Viva La Vida
ARTIST
Coldplay
YEAR
2008

SONGSPIRATION CONTEXT

The band said that the song's name was inspired by a phrase found in a drawing by the great Mexican artist Frida Kahlo. „Viva la Vida“ has its origin in Spanish and means something like „long live life“ or „live life“. ¡Sí, señores!

FEATURED FONTS

Each created in the year of the song release (from top to bottom, left to right)

Calypso, Aviano serif

Classified and available through
identifont.com

Design: i_dbuero × OA Krimmel
Celebrating: Remo Eric Vermont

Everybody
Everybody
dance
dance
Now

APRIL

SONG
Gonna Make You Sweat (Everybody Dance Now)

ARTIST
C & C Music Factory

YEAR
1990

SONGSPIRATION CONTEXT
Today is 'International Dance Day'. "This day is a celebration day for those who can see the value and importance of the art form 'dance', and acts as a wake-up call for governments, politicians and institutions which have not yet recognised its value to the people and to the individual and have not yet realised its potential for economic growth." Or you simply dance.

FEATURED FONTS
Each created in the year of the song release (from top to bottom, left to right)

ITC Bolt

Classified and available through identifont.com

Design: i_dbuero × OA Krimmel

Don't give up

APRIL

SONG
Don't Give Up
ARTIST
Peter Gabriel & Kate Bush
YEAR
1986

SONGSPIRATION CONTEXT

Peter Gabriel has revealed that Dolly Parton was his first choice to sing on his classic single 'Don't Give Up' – and that Kate Bush was only drafted in as her replacement. He said he was "glad" that Bush had ended up taking singing duties for the track instead of the country legend.

FEATURED FONTS

Each created in the year of the song release (from top to bottom, left to right)

Forest Shaded Plain

Classified and available through identifont.com

Design: i_dbuero × Evelyn Binder

GET UP,
STAND UP
STAND UP
FOR YOUR
RIGHTS

1

MAY

SONG
Get Up, Stand Up
ARTIST
Bob Marley & The Wailers
YEAR
1973

SONGSPIRATION CONTEXT

The International Workers Day, also known as Labour Day, in most countries is a celebration of labourers and the working classes. It occurs every year on May Day (1 May).
Get up, stand up.

FEATURED FONTS

Each created in the year of the song release (from top to bottom, left to right)

Eksell Sans, Maximus BT

Classified and available through identifont.com

Design: i_dbuero × Carsten Güth

GET UP,
STAND UP
DON'T GIVE UP
THE FIGHT

SONG
Get Up, Stand Up

ARTIST
Bob Marley & The Wailers

YEAR
1973

SONGSPIRATION CONTEXT

This was the last song Bob Marley performed; he sang it from a stool at a show in Pittsburgh. Marley's cancer had spread to his brain and it was surprising he could perform at all, but he did a 20-song set that night, closing with a 6-minute rendition of 'Get Up, Stand Up', and collapsing soon after the show. He would die on May 11, 1981.

FEATURED FONTS

Each created in the year of the song release (from top to bottom, left to right)

Eksell Sans, Maximus BT

Classified and available through identifont.com

Design: i_dbuero × Carsten Güth

LISTEN AS YOUR

UNFOLDS

SONG
You Gotta Be
ARTIST
Des'ree
YEAR
1994

SONGSPIRATION CONTEXT

"We have two ears and only one tongue in order that we may listen more and speak less."
(Diogenes Laertios, born 180 CE)

FEATURED FONTS

Each created in the year of the song release (from top to bottom, left to right)

Gusto

Classified and available through identifont.com

Design: i_dbuero × Carsten Güth

You don't know the power of the dark side

SONG
The Imperial March (Star Wars Cover)

ARTIST
Celldweller

YEAR
2015

SONGSPIRATION CONTEXT

Star Wars Day is an informal commemorative day observed annually on May 4 to celebrate George Lucas *Star Wars*. The date originated from the pun 'May the Fourth be with you', a variant of the world-famous *Star Wars* catchphrase, our calendar motto for you today – and still: "May the Force be with you!"

FEATURED FONTS

Each created in the year of the song release (from top to bottom, left to right)

Classified and available through identifont.com

Design: i_dbuero × Jan Michalski

5

MAY

SONG
Someone like You
ARTIST
Adele
YEAR
2011

SONGSPIRATION CONTEXT

Happy Birthday Adele, born in 1988.
"It's simple – just letting go. It makes me really upset. It's my most articulate song. It's just to the point, it's not trying to be clever, I think that's why I like it so much, because it's just so honest, no glitter on it."
(Adele in an interview to *The Sun*)

FEATURED FONTS

Each created in the year of the song release (from top to bottom, left to right)

Ostrich Sans, Battlefin

Classified and available through identifont.com

Design: i_dbuero × Carsten Güth

i just want to *LIVE* while i'm *ALIVE*

SONG
It's My Life
ARTIST
Bon Jovi
YEAR
2000

SONGSPIRATION CONTEXT

Bon Jovi were originally going to name themselves Johnny Electric ... that is until a friend suggested they follow Van Halen's example and take their lead singer's name. Whose real name actually is John Francis Bongiovi jr.! His father was of Italian and Slovak ancestry, and his mother was of German and Russian descent.

FEATURED FONTS

Each created in the year of the song release (from top to bottom, left to right)

Geo

Classified and available through identifont.com

Design: i_dbuero × Hanna Spitznagel

Niemand niemand
kann's dir kann's dir
SAGEN
Keiner keiner kennt die
ANTWORT
ANTWORT
Auf alle alle deine deine
FRAGEN

SONG
Ernten was wir säen
ARTIST
Die Fantastischen Vier
YEAR
1997

SONGSPIRATION CONTEXT

On 7 May 1989, independent election observers were able to prove that the results of the local elections in the GDR had been manipulated. When the election director Egon Krenz announced the official result, 98.85 percent yes votes for the SED, the population reacted to the fraud with resentment and demonstrations. Six months later, the Wall finally and definitively fell.

FEATURED FONTS

Each created in the year of the song release (from top to bottom, left to right)

Atrament, Glow Gothic

Classified and available through identifont.com

Design: i_dbuero × Carsten Güth

Und die
Sonne
geht auf,
und die
Erde
geht
unter

SONG
Der Mond

ARTIST
Rocko Schamoni / LaBrassBanda

YEAR
1999/2014

SONGSPIRATION CONTEXT

Great songline “Even Armstrong only stirred me up on the outside”. Great (song)writer King Rocko Schamoni. It's his birthday today, Hail to the King!

FEATURED FONTS

Each created in the year of the song release (from top to bottom, left to right)

Selfie

Classified and available through identifont.com

Design: i_dbuero × OA Krimmel

We
can be
HEROES
just for
one day

9

MAY

SONG
Heroes
ARTIST
David Bowie
YEAR
1977

SONGSPIRATION CONTEXT

"I'm allowed to talk about it now. I wasn't at the time. I always said it was a couple of lovers by the Berlin Wall that prompted the idea. Actually, it was [producer] Tony Visconti and his girlfriend. Tony was married at the time. And I could never say who it was (laughs). But I can now say that the lovers were Tony and a German girl that he'd met whilst we were in Berlin." (David Bowie, 2003)

FEATURED FONTS

Each created in the year of the song release (from top to bottom, left to right)

ITC Fenice

Classified and available through identifont.com

Design: i_dbuero × Sabine Schneider

Did you ever know that you're my

SONG
Wind Beneath My Wings

ARTIST
Bette Midler

YEAR
1988

SONGSPIRATION CONTEXT

The most famous version of this song was Bette Midler's, who recorded it in 1988 for the movie *Beaches*, in which she starred. It appears in a dramatic scene at the end of the film after the character played by Barbara Hershey dies. After Midler's version became a hit, many other artists recorded the song, including Willie Nelson, John Tesh, Patti LaBelle, Perry Como and Judy Collins. It is one of the most performed songs of all time. (songfacts.com)

FEATURED FONTS

Each created in the year of the song release (from top to bottom, left to right)

Tropical, Avenir, Laser Chrome

Classified and available through identifont.com

Design: i_dbuero × Carsten Güth

Where
Are
Those
Happy
Days

SONG
S.O.S.
ARTIST
ABBA
YEAR
1975

SONGSPIRATION CONTEXT

In 1979 ABBA were on tour in the USA. They flew from New York to Boston in a private jet – but a tornado hit and put the band and crew in real danger. They sent out an S.O.S. before finally managing to land at the nearest airport. The fright was so great that Agnetha never set foot on a plane again.

FEATURED FONTS

Each created in the year of the song release (from top to bottom, left to right)

Tango

Classified and available through identifont.com

Design: i_dbuero × OA Krimmel

Mah
Nà
Mah
Nà

MAY

SONG
Mah Nà Mah Nà
ARTIST
Piero Umiliani / Cover: The Muppets
YEAR
1968

SONGSPIRATION CONTEXT

Known around the world as a hilarious Muppets song, this catchy tune was composed by Piero Umiliani. He wrote it originally for the salacious movie *Sweden: Heaven and Hell*, which was a documentary about the sexual habits of Scandinavians. When the song plays in the film, we see a group of beautiful women enter a sauna. Got the picture?!

FEATURED FONTS

Each created in the year of the song release (from top to bottom, left to right)

Fontella

Classified and available through identifont.com

Design: i_dbuero × OA Krimmel

What a day for a daydream

13

MAY

SONG
Daydream
ARTIST
The Lovin' Spoonful
YEAR
1965

SONGSPIRATION CONTEXT

The name of the band is officially inspired by the song by Mississippi John Hurt called 'Coffee Blues'. In it, he describes a Maxwell coffee as being so good that he only needs a spoonful of it to feel good, which he calls "my lovin' spoonful" in the song.

FEATURED FONTS

Each created in the year of the song release (from top to bottom, left to right)

Harry Plain & Harry Obese

Classified and available through identifont.com

Design: i_dbuero × Christoph Binder

Don't lose your grip on the dreams of the past

14

MAY

SONG
Eye of the Tiger

ARTIST
Survivor

YEAR
1982

SONGSPIRATION CONTEXT

Already the opening sequence gets you going. A favorite motivational song for athletes, certainly because it's the theme song for *Rocky III*. "Whether you need to tackle a huge flight of stairs (like Rocky), clean the house, or get pumped for your next marathon, Survivor is a great place to start." (Natalie Seale)

FEATURED FONTS

Each created in the year of the song release (from top to bottom, left to right)

Crillee

Classified and available through identifont.com

Design: i_dbuero × Syl Hillier

there
can 
be
miracles

SONG
When You Believe
ARTIST
Whitney Houston & Mariah Carey
YEAR
1998

SONGSPIRATION CONTEXT

The song line from the animated film musical *The Prince Of Egypt* does not only apply to princes, pharaohs, bunnies or ... guinea pigs. It is actually quite a miracle that you are able to read this text today. Because after all, it took about 6 million years of human evolution and an immense number of other miraculous *coincidences* for you to be standing here today in front of this calendar sheet.

FEATURED FONTS

Each created in the year of the song release (from top to bottom, left to right)

Aura Oblique

Classified and available through identifont.com

Design: i_dbuero × OA Krimmel

SMILE

WHAT'S THE USE OF CRYING

SONG
Smile
ARTIST
Charlie Chaplin
YEAR
1936/1954

SONGSPIRATION CONTEXT

'Smile' is a song by Charlie Chaplin, which he initially composed without lyrics for his classic film *Modern Times*. The melody initially remained without the now familiar lyrics until 1954, when the songwriting duo Turner/Parsons added them. With these new lyrics, Chaplin's song became a chart success through Nat King Cole's interpretation. The very first Oscar® ceremony took place on this day (in 1929) and Charlie Chaplin received the 'Honorary Award' in 1972.

FEATURED FONTS

Each created in the year of the song release (from top to bottom, left to right)

AFT Headline Gothic

Classified and available through identifont.com

Design: i_dbuero × Hanna Spitznagel

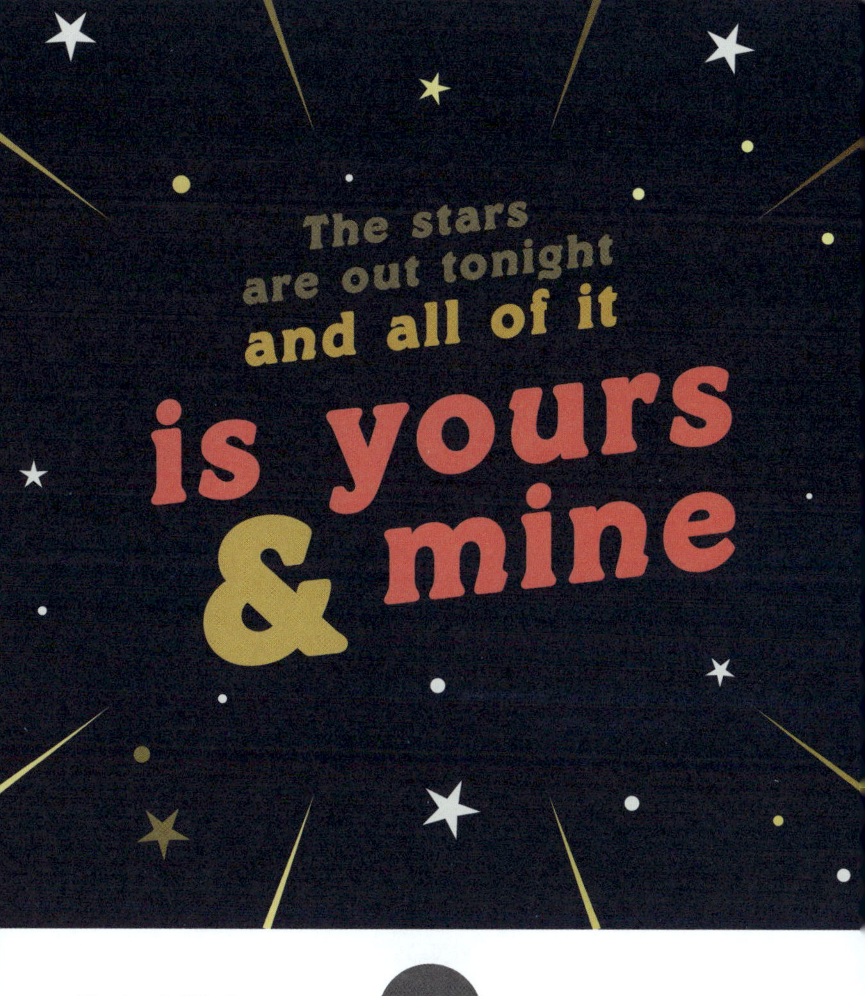
The stars
are out tonight
and all of it
is yours
& mine

SONG
The Passenger
ARTIST
Iggy Pop
YEAR
1977

SONGSPIRATION CONTEXT

Iggy Pop wrote this song in the *S-Bahn* of Berlin. He remembered in 2008 how he and David Bowie still had to do the everyday things during their *exile* in Berlin: "Living in a Berlin apartment with Bowie and his friends was interesting. Who did the chores? Well, I seem to remember doing a little hoovering. The big event of the week was Thursday night. Anyone who was still alive and able to crawl to the sofa would watch *Starsky & Hutch*."

FEATURED FONTS

Each created in the year of the song release (from top to bottom, left to right)

Paddington

Classified and available through identifont.com

Design: i_dbuero × Sabine Schneider

Black hole
SUN
won't
you come

SONG
Black Hole Sun
ARTIST
Soundgarden
YEAR
1994

SONGSPIRATION CONTEXT

The most probable fate of our planet is absorption by the Sun in about 7.5 billion years, after the star has entered the red giant phase and expanded beyond the planet's current orbit. The Soundgarden frontman was just 52 years old when he sealed his fate on May 18 in 2017 by suicide – after being depressed and consuming a cocktail of drugs.

FEATURED FONTS

Each created in the year of the song release (from top to bottom, left to right)

Inky Black

Classified and available through identifont.com

Design: i_dbuero × Carsten Güth

WANN STRAHLST DU?

SONG
Wann strahlst Du?

ARTIST
Erobique & Jacques Palminger

YEAR
2007

SONGSPIRATION CONTEXT

Ich liebe die Träumer, die Aufbruchsgeister / Die überall Samen erkennen / Die Fehlschläge nicht zu ernst nehmen / Und immer das Gute benennen / Nicht die, die die Zukunft auswendig kennen / Begeisterung als Naivität anschauen / Und dir ihre altbekannten Ängste / Als Ratschläge verpackt um die Ohren hauen / Ich schulde dem Leben das Leuchten in meinen Augen Wann strahlst du?

FEATURED FONTS

Each created in the year of the song release (from top to bottom, left to right)

Flap Jacks NF, Guillotine, Supersquared

Classified and available through identifont.com

Design: i_dbuero × Carsten Güth

BIRDS

do it,

BEES

do it, even educated

FLEAS

do it

MAY

SONG
Let's Do It
ARTIST
Cole Porter (Ella Fitzgerald Version)
YEAR
1928

SONGSPIRATION CONTEXT

Let's go. Let's fall in love with the bees. Fittingly, today is World Bee Day. A little love incentive: For one jar (500 g) of honey, bees fly a distance of about 120,000 kilometers on average, which corresponds to three circumnavigations of the earth! If that's not enough, bees are mankind's most important useful animal thanks to their pollination.

FEATURED FONTS

Each created in the year of the song release (from top to bottom, left to right)

Modernique, Bodoni No.1

Classified and available through identifont.com

Design: i_dbuero × Martin Drozmann

IT´S LIKE A JUNGLE SOMETIMES.

SONG
The Message
ARTIST
Grandmaster Flash and The Furious Five
YEAR
1982

SONGSPIRATION CONTEXT
“Where it was inarguably innovative, was in slowing the beat right down, and opening up space in the instrumentation – the music isn't so much hip-hop as noirish, nightmarish slow-funk, stifling and claustrophobic, with electro, dub and disco also jostling for room in the genre mix – and thereby letting the lyrics speak loud and clear.” (The Sunday Times)

FEATURED FONTS
Each created in the year of the song release (from top to bottom, left to right)

Van Dijk Bold

Classified and available through identifont.com

Design: i_dbuero × Martin Drozmann

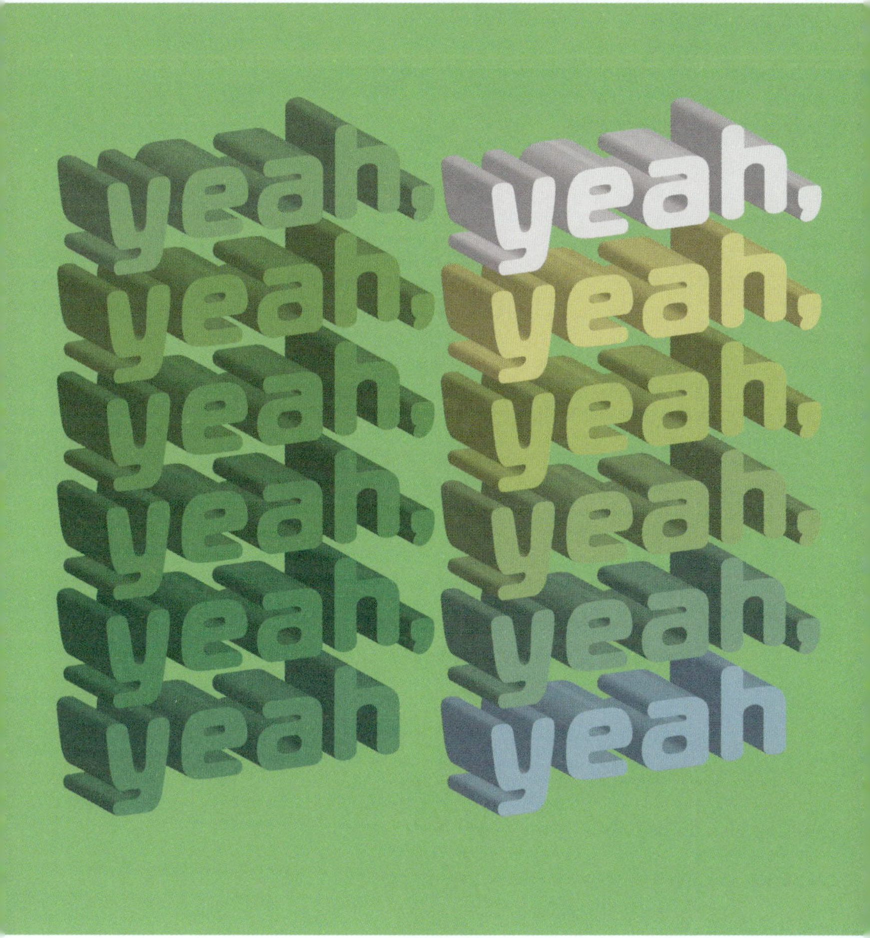

yeah, yeah,
yeah, yeah,
yeah, yeah,
yeah, yeah,
yeah, yeah,
yeah yeah

MAY

SONG
Yeah!
ARTIST
Usher
YEAR
2004

SONGSPIRATION CONTEXT

'Yeah!' went to #1 in the US on February 2004 and stayed there until May 22 (12 weeks), when it was replaced by his next single, 'Burn', which held the top spot another eight weeks. This was the first time a song with a four-letter title replaced another at #1.

FEATURED FONTS

Each created in the year of the song release (from top to bottom, left to right)

Biortech

Classified and available through identifont.com

Design: i_dbuero × OA Krimmel

23

MAY

SONG
You Gotta Be
ARTIST
Des'ree
YEAR
1994

SONGSPIRATION CONTEXT

As a result of the romantic transfiguration of the story of the wandering and hunted gangster couple, the term “like Bonnie and Clyde” has become proverbial for inseparability in the face of adverse circumstances, for unbreakable love and cohesion even in death (better dead than separated or trapped) and for “it's you and me against the world”. On 23 May 1934, the bank robber couple was riddled with 100 rounds of ammunition by police.

FEATURED FONTS

Each created in the year of the song release (from top to bottom, left to right)

Soraya

Classified and available through identifont.com

Design: i_dbuero × Syl Hillier

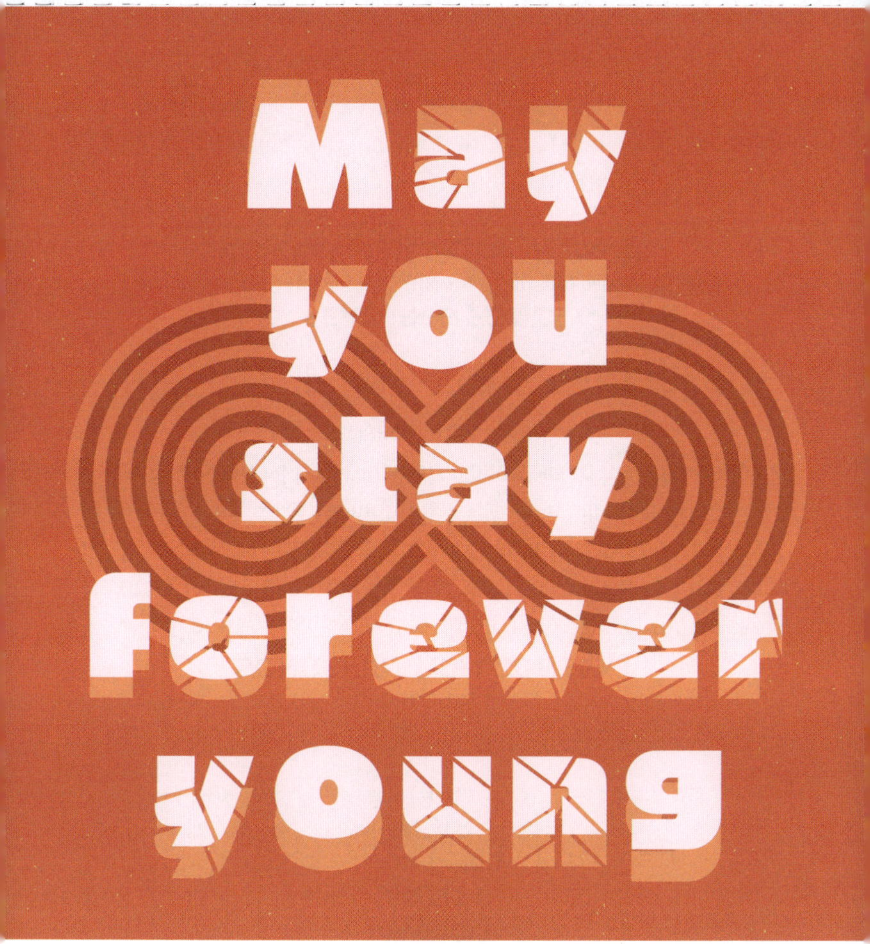

May you stay forever young

MAY

SONG
Forever Young
ARTIST
Bob Dylan
YEAR
1974

SONGSPIRATION CONTEXT

May is pretty exclusive when it comes to days of the week. No other month in one single year starts or finishes on the same weekday as May. Basically, if May 1 is on a Friday, and the May 31 is on a Sunday, no other months in the year will start or end on a Friday or a Sunday! Bob Dylan officially started his life on May 24 in the year 1941, a Saturday.

FEATURED FONTS

Each created in the year of the song release (from top to bottom, left to right)

Baby Cakes NF, BigbandTerrazzo

Classified and available through identifont.com

Design: i_dbuero × Evelyn Binder

Baby, it ain't over 'til it's OVER

25

MAY

SONG
It Ain't Over 'Til It's Over
ARTIST
Lenny Kravitz
YEAR
1991

SONGSPIRATION CONTEXT

Kravitz wrote this about the actress Lisa Bonet. They got married in 1987 and had a daughter, Zoe, a year later. But in 1991, their marriage was on the rocks, and Kravitz wrote 'It Ain't Over 'Til It's Over' hoping to reconcile their relationship. They ended up getting divorced in 1993, but later became good friends. (songfacts.com)

FEATURED FONTS

Each created in the year of the song release (from top to bottom, left to right)

Rockwell, Compact Broken

Classified and available through identifont.com

Design: i_dbuero × Carsten Güth

THE WORLD IS A VAMPIRE

26

MAY

SONG
Bullet with Butterfly Wings

ARTIST
The Smashing Pumpkins

YEAR
1995

SONGSPIRATION CONTEXT

... or the other way round:
today is World Vampire Day!

FEATURED FONTS

Each created in the year of the song release (from top to bottom, left to right)

ITC Airstream

Classified and available through
identifont.com

Design: i_dbuero × Sabine Schneider

CAUSE IT'S A

bitter

sweet

SYMPHONY,

that's life

SONG
Bitter Sweet Symphony
ARTIST
The Verve
YEAR
1997

SONGSPIRATION CONTEXT
The famous orchestral riff incorporates a sample from an obscure instrumental version of the Rolling Stones song 'The Last Time' by Stones producer Andrew Loog Oldham, who included it on a 1966 album called *The Rolling Stones Songbook*. (songfacts.com)

FEATURED FONTS
Each created in the year of the song release (from top to bottom, left to right)

DIN Condensed, Grapefruit ITC, Carnation

Classified and available through identifont.com

Design: i_dbuero × Carsten Güth

YES, IT'S A GOOD DAY FOR SINGIN' A SONG

SONG
It's a Good Day
ARTIST
Peggy Lee
YEAR
1950

SONGSPIRATION CONTEXT

When Bing Crosby's iconic "White Christmas" came out, it was welcomed as readily as a sleigh full of gifts, becoming one of the most successful songs in the history of recorded music. (With 50,000,000 copies sold, the Guinness Book of World Records dubs it the best-selling single of all time). On this day (in 1942) he recorded it in the studio.

FEATURED FONTS

Each created in the year of the song release (from top to bottom, left to right)

Festival Titling

Classified and available through
identifont.com

Design: i_dbuero × Evelyn Binder

This is gonna be the

best day of my life

29

MAY

SONG
Best Day Of My Life

ARTIST
American Authors

YEAR
2014

SONGSPIRATION CONTEXT

When was the best day of your life?

Or is it yet to come?

You decide ...

FEATURED FONTS

Each created in the year of the song release (from top to bottom, left to right)

Aguda

Classified and available through identifont.com

Design: i_dbuero × Evelyn Binder

shine on
you crazy
diamond

30

MAY

SONG
Shine On You Crazy Diamond
ARTIST
Pink Floyd
YEAR
1975

SONGSPIRATION CONTEXT

The song is a tribute to former band member Syd Barrett, hence the opening words 'Shine On You Crazy Diamond'. He was the lead guitarist in the beginning and wrote the first hits, but drug use and mental illness led to his kicking out of the band. During the recording of this song he suddenly appeared in the studio after years, "he was fat, bald, had shaved eyebrows and was crazy as they remembered him".

FEATURED FONTS

Each created in the year of the song release (from top to bottom, left to right)

Knightsbride

Classified and available through identifont.com

Design: i_dbuero × Sabine Schneider

supercalifragilisticexpialidocious

SONG
supercalifragilisticexpialidocious
ARTIST
Julie Andrews, Dick Van Dyke, The Pearly Chorus
YEAR
1964

SONGSPIRATION CONTEXT

During this Disney musical song, Mary Poppins says, "You know, you can say it backwards, which is *dociousaliexpilistic-fragilcalirupus*', but that's going a bit too far, don't you think?" (To which Dick Van Dyke replies, "Indubitably.")

FEATURED FONTS

Each created in the year of the song release (from top to bottom, left to right)

Sabon

Classified and available through identifont.com

Design: i_dbuero × Suse W

is what happens

LIFE

to you

while you're busy

making

other plans

1

JUNE

SONG
Beautiful Boy
ARTIST
John Lennon
YEAR
1980

SONGSPIRATION CONTEXT

Today is World Children's Day. John Lennon wrote this song for the child he had with Yoko Ono. "You can't give a child too much love and if you love somebody, you can't be with them enough. There's no such thing." (John Lennon)

FEATURED FONTS

Each created in the year of the song release (from top to bottom, left to right)

Baskerville

Classified and available through identifont.com

Design: i_dbuero × OA Krimmel

you gotta fight

for your right

SONG
Fight For Your Right
ARTIST
Beastie Boys
YEAR
1986

SONGSPIRATION CONTEXT

Fight for your right to know mad trivia: *Beastie* Boys is an acronym for *Boys Entering Anarchistic Stages Towards Inner Excellence.* And now: Paaaaarty!

FEATURED FONTS

Each created in the year of the song release (from top to bottom, left to right)

ITC Eras, Insignia, Freestyle Script, Bronx

Classified and available through identifont.com

Design: i_dbuero × Thomas Hofmann

IT´S A SLOW DAY WITHOUT YOU

SONG
Slow Day
ARTIST
Die Happy
YEAR
2003

SONGSPIRATION CONTEXT

"Three films a day, three books a week and records of great music would be enough to make me happy to the day I die."
(François Truffaut)

FEATURED FONTS

Each created in the year of the song release (from top to bottom, left to right)

Boler

Classified and available through
identifont.com

Design: i_dbuero × Ralph Rieker

You always had it, but you never knew.

4

JUNE

SONG
Flesh and Bone
ARTIST
The Killers
YEAR
2012

SONGSPIRATION CONTEXT
“Early Killers lyrics were biting and melancholy, but as they’ve matured they’ve included some uplift among the sass and sadness. People will break your heart, Brandon assures us, but they won’t break the fight inside of us.”
(the talking llama)

FEATURED FONTS
Each created in the year of the song release (from top to bottom, left to right)

Askan

Classified and available through identifont.com

Design: i_dbuero × Sabine Schneider

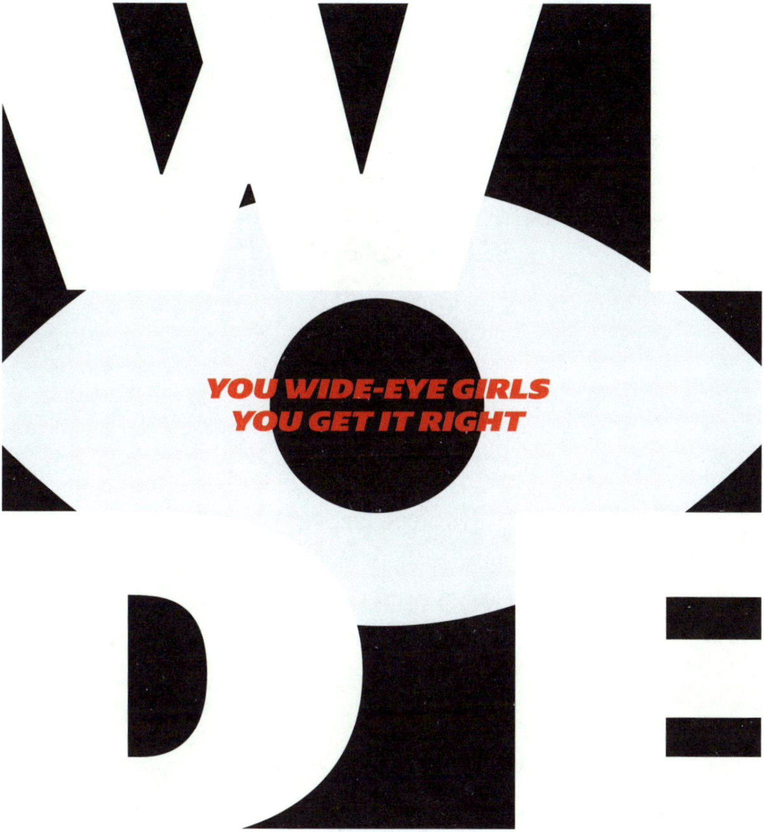

YOU WIDE-EYE GIRLS
YOU GET IT RIGHT

JUNE

SONG
Seraphim
ARTIST
For Today
YEAR
2010

SONGSPIRATION CONTEXT

"What matters most is how well you walk through the fire."
(Charles Bukowski)

FEATURED FONTS

Each created in the year of the song release (from top to bottom, left to right)

Ebony

Classified and available through
identifont.com

Design: i_dbuero × Hanna Spitznagel

WHAT IS IT GOOD FOR?

Absolutely nothing

JUNE

SONG
War
ARTIST
Edwin Starr
YEAR
1970

SONGSPIRATION CONTEXT

Today marks the anniversary of historic D-Day. The successful landing of the Allies in Normandy ended the cruel Second World War. 'War' is one of the most famous anti-war songs and was written because of the Vietnam War. It belongs to 'the list of 500 songs that most influenced rock and roll'. Numerous cover versions, including those by Bruce Springsteen and *Frankie Goes to Hollywood*, underline this.

FEATURED FONTS

Each created in the year of the song release (from top to bottom, left to right)

ITC Pioneer, ITC Grouch

Classified and available through identifont.com

Design: i_dbuero × Katrin Schlüsener

Dearly beloved,
we are gathered
here today to
get through this
thing called
Life

7

JUNE

SONG
Let's Go Crazy
ARTIST
Prince and The Revolution
YEAR
1984

SONGSPIRATION CONTEXT

What should we do when we suspect that our great love is cheating on us?! Go absolutely crazy, of course! The artist formerly (between 1993 and 2000) called 'the artist formerly known as Prince' has hidden the right tip in this song: "Look for the purple banana / Until they put us in the truck." Nothing to add. Except it's his birthday today (1958).

FEATURED FONTS

Each created in the year of the song release (from top to bottom, left to right)

Rage Italic

Classified and available through identifont.com

Design: i_dbuero × Syl Hillier

WE ARE ALL
HUMAN,

IT'S TIME TO
PROVE IT

JUNE

SONG
911 For Peace
ARTIST
Anti-Flag
YEAR
2002

SONGSPIRATION CONTEXT

The band claims that their number one goal is to break down artificial barriers between different groups of people. Members are often quoted as saying that Anti-Flag are not a skin color, religious preference, sexual orientation, or anything of the sort: they're simply human beings, and it's this message that they hope to spread to fans across the world. (songfacts.com)

FEATURED FONTS

Each created in the year of the song release (from top to bottom, left to right)

SB Basement

Classified and available through identifont.com

Design: i_dbuero × Tim Oliver Schweizer

9

JUNE

SONG
Birthday Cake
ARTIST
Rihanna
YEAR
2011

SONGSPIRATION CONTEXT

Rihanna has made millions from her music, but that's chump change compared to what she earns with her beauty line, Fenty (her real name is Robyn Fenty). In 2021, *Forbes* estimated her net worth at $1.7 billion, far more than any other female musician. About $1.4 billion of that is from Fenty Beauty, which sells makeup and skin care products. (songfacts.com)

FEATURED FONTS

Each created in the year of the song release (from top to bottom, left to right)

Dimensions 700, Damion

Classified and available through identifont.com

Design: i_dbuero × Carsten Güth

10

JUNE

SONG
Stressed Out
ARTIST
Twenty One Pilots
YEAR
2015

SONGSPIRATION CONTEXT

The band name also serves as a credo for the duo: In the Arthur Miller play *All My Sons*, a World War II contractor delivers defective airplane parts because fixing the error will be expensive. As a result, 21 pilots are killed. The story reminds Joseph and Dun that they should avoid shortcuts and act with integrity. (songfacts.com)

FEATURED FONTS

Each created in the year of the song release (from top to bottom, left to right)

Sanomat Sans Black

Classified and available through identifont.com

Design: i_dbuero × Evelyn Binder

Get your Freak on

JUNE

SONG
Get ur Freak on

ARTIST
Missy Elliott

YEAR
2001

SONGSPIRATION CONTEXT

"It could be about dancing – the bedroom, whatever. You're cleaning your house? Get your freak on!" (Missy Elliott, 2007)

FEATURED FONTS

Each created in the year of the song release (from top to bottom, left to right)

Saturday Night

Classified and available through identifont.com

Design: i_dbuero × Carsten Güth

Für mich soll´s
rote Rosen
regnen

SONG
Für mich soll's rote Rosen regnen
ARTIST
Hildegard Knef
YEAR
1968

SONGSPIRATION CONTEXT

Dia dos Namorados (June 12): In Brazil, the *dia dos Namorados*, literally translates to 'Lovers Day'. Couples exchange gifts, chocolates, cards and flower bouquets. Valentine's Day usually falls within Brazil's carnival and is not celebrated.

FEATURED FONTS

Each created in the year of the song release (from top to bottom, left to right)

Geo

Classified and available through
identifont.com

Design: i_dbuero × Hanna Spitznagel

There is a Light that never goes out

SONG
There Is a Light That Never Goes Out

ARTIST
The Smiths

YEAR
1986

SONGSPIRATION CONTEXT
"I didn't realise that 'There Is A Light That Never Goes Out' was going to be an anthem but when we first played it I thought it was the best song I'd ever heard."

(Guitarist Johnny Marr)

FEATURED FONTS
Each created in the year of the song release (from top to bottom, left to right)

Cantoria MT

Classified and available through identifont.com

Design: i_dbuero × Carsten Güth

I,
I follow,
I follow
you

14

JUNE

SONG
I Follow Rivers
ARTIST
Lykke Li
YEAR
2011

SONGSPIRATION CONTEXT

"You know when you're kind of into it really badly, you're in some kind of destructive situation, very unbalanced. You're driven by desire, and desire can lead you into a very dark place, whether it be drugs or love, and it's kind of like you're powerless."
(Lykke Li about the song's meaning)

FEATURED FONTS

Each created in the year of the song release (from top to bottom, left to right)

Akko Pro

Classified and available through
identifont.com

Design: i_dbuero × Syl Hillier

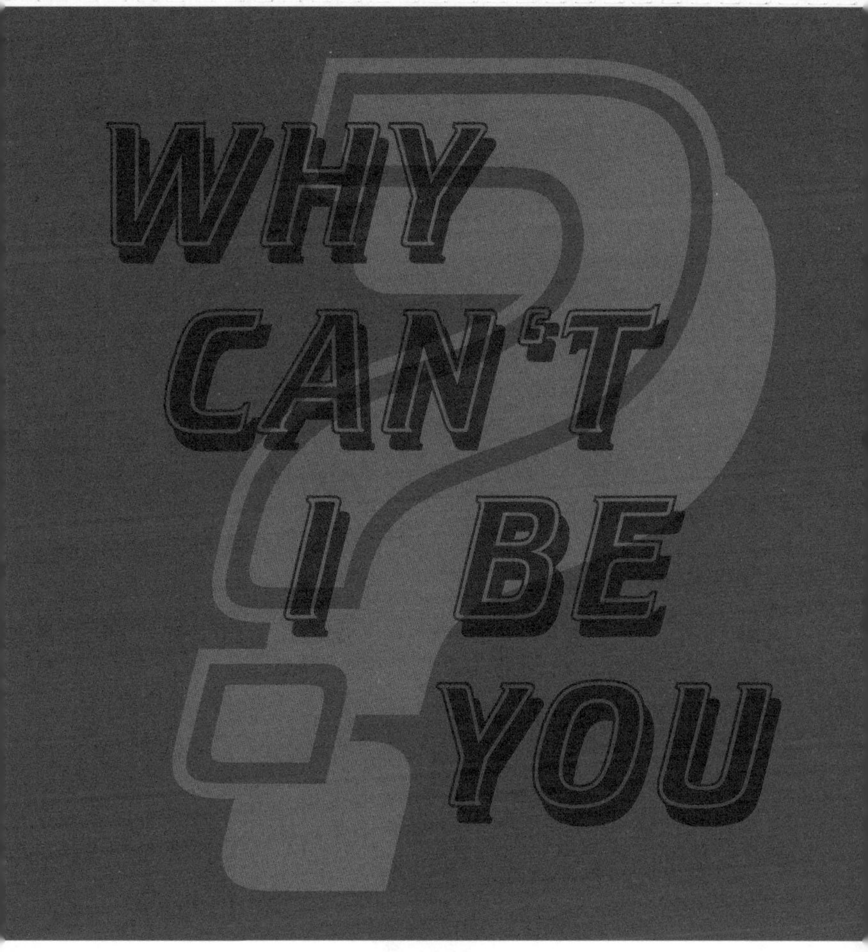

WHY CAN'T I BE YOU

JUNE

SONG
Why Can't I Be You?
ARTIST
The Cure
YEAR
1987

SONGSPIRATION CONTEXT

The Cure's frontman Robert Smith created this song because a fan wrote him this exact line. In 1987, millions of teenagers would certainly have loved to swap places with the charismatic singer. But Robert himself also fancied someone back then; namely his childhood sweetheart Mary Poole, whom he then married the following year. Apparently even better than being someone else is to live together with that someone.

FEATURED FONTS

Each created in the year of the song release (from top to bottom, left to right)

Crillee Italic Shadow

Classified and available through identifont.com

Design: i_dbuero × OA Krimmel

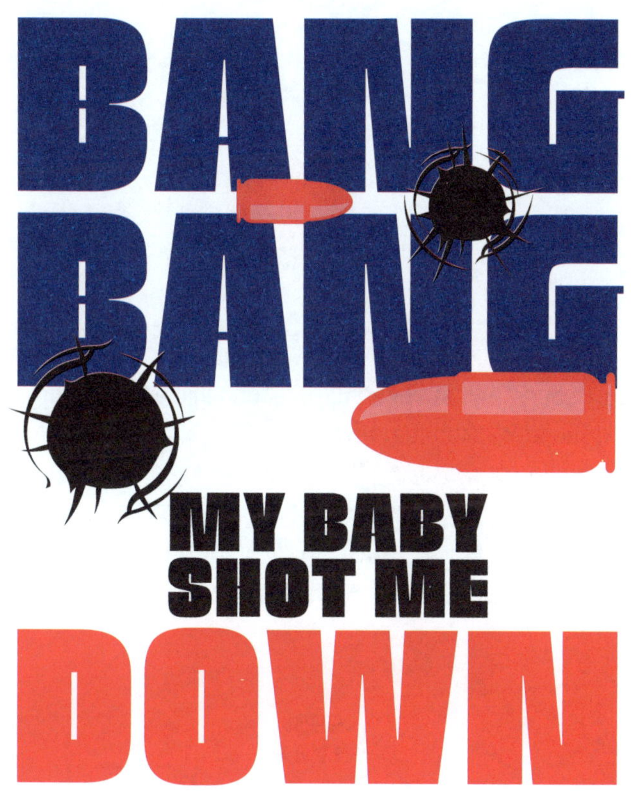
BANG
BANG
MY BABY
SHOT ME
DOWN

SONG

Bang Bang (My Baby Shot Me Down)

ARTIST

Nancy Sinatra (Original: Cher)

YEAR

1966

SONGSPIRATION CONTEXT

Nancy Sinatra's version is certainly the best known, thanks in no small part to Quentin Tarantino's *Kill Bill*, which used the song in its opening credits 37 years later. However the original is by Cher, but the song exists in many different cover versions - from Frank Sinatra to Vanilla Fudge, from Dalida to Lady Gaga – check out her live version, BANG!

FEATURED FONTS

Each created in the year of the song release (from top to bottom, left to right)

Neil

Classified and available through identifont.com

Design: i_dbuero × Carsten Güth

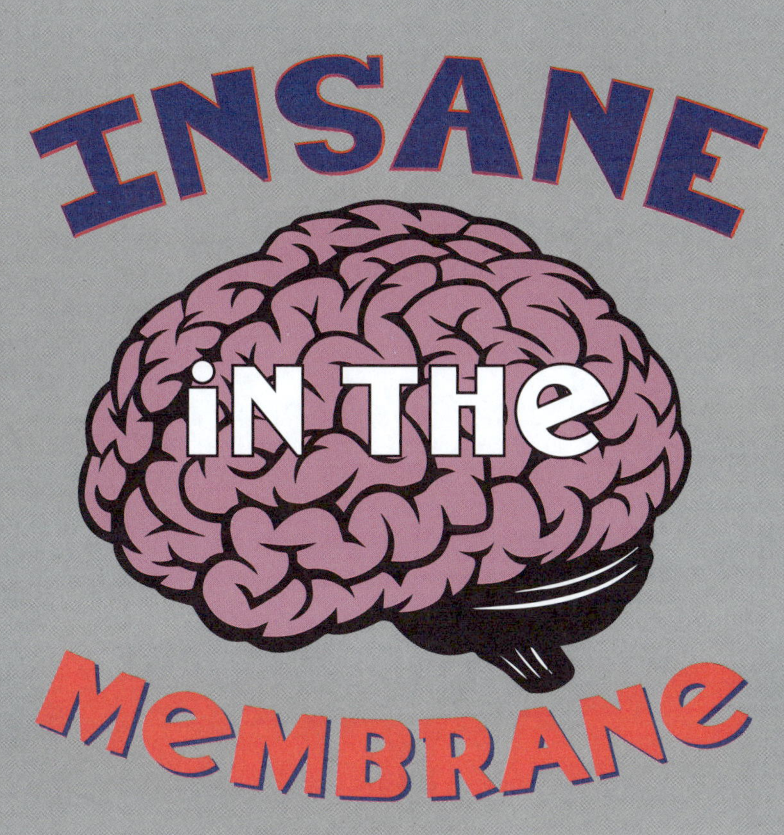
INSANE
IN THE
MEMBRANE

SONG
Insane In The Brain
ARTIST
Cypress Hill
YEAR
1966

SONGSPIRATION CONTEXT

Dreaming permits each and every one of us to be quietly and safely insane every night of the week.
(William Dement)

FEATURED FONTS

Each created in the year of the song release (from top to bottom, left to right)

Bad Typ

Classified and available through identifont.com

Design: i_dbuero × Carsten Güth

There are places I'll remember
All my
Life

SONG
In My Life
ARTIST
The Beatles
YEAR
1965

SONGSPIRATION CONTEXT

Today in 1942, Paul McCartney was born in Liverpool at 20 Forthlin Road. It is the house in which he lived for several years and it is labelled officially by the National Trust as 'the birthplace of the Beatles'.

FEATURED FONTS

Each created in the year of the song release (from top to bottom, left to right)

Social Gothic

Classified and available through identifont.com

Design: i_dbuero × OA Krimmel

WHERE HEARTS
WERE ENTERTAINING JUNE
WE STOOD BENEATH
AN AMBER MOON
AND SOFTLY MURMURED

"SOMEDAY SOON"

SONG
Brazil
ARTIST
Geoff & Maria Muldaur
YEAR
1970

SONGSPIRATION CONTEXT

Geoff and his then wife Maria Muldaur recorded their first album, *Pottery Pie*, for Warner Bros. Records. This album contained the version of 'Brazil' ('Aquarela do Brasil'), which became the theme for the film *Brazil* directed by Terry Gilliam.

FEATURED FONTS

Each created in the year of the song release (from top to bottom, left to right)

ITC Avant Garde

Classified and available through identifont.com

Design: i_dbuero × SB

I GOT YOU

moonlight

YOU'RE MY

starlight

SONG
Levitating
ARTIST
Dua Lipa
YEAR
2020

SONGSPIRATION CONTEXT

"It's about having fun and meeting someone and falling in love and thinking, You've probably met me at the perfect time, let's just go for it ... It's the feeling when love makes you feel like you're levitating. It's otherworldly." (Dua Lipa)

FEATURED FONTS

Each created in the year of the song release (from top to bottom, left to right)

Ginto Nord, Nordeco Cyrillic

Classified and available through identifont.com

Design: i_dbuero × Caroline Glock

LET YOUR BODY MOVE TO THE MUSIC

JUNE

SONG
Vogue
ARTIST
Madonna
YEAR
1990

SONGSPIRATION CONTEXT

Today is summer solstice! It marks the beginning of the summer season in the Northern Hemisphere. On this day, solar radiation in the Northern Hemisphere is the longest in the year. On this day SONGSPIRATION suggests some Vogueing to charm a great summer.

FEATURED FONTS

Each created in the year of the song release (from top to bottom, left to right)

Geometric 415

Classified and available through identifont.com

Design: i_dbuero × Caroline Glock

The Time of my Life

22

JUNE

SONG

(I've had) the Time of My Life

ARTIST

Bill Medley, Jennifer Warnes

YEAR

1987

SONGSPIRATION CONTEXT

Today in 1986, Argentine football (soccer) player Diego Maradona scored his memorable *Hand of God* goal (the ball struck his hand, but the referee mistakenly thought it had hit his head) to help Argentina defeat England in a World Cup quarter-final game; Argentina went on to win the tournament.

FEATURED FONTS

Each created in the year of the song release (from top to bottom, left to right)

Laser

Classified and available through identifont.com

Design: i_dbuero × Suse W

Not today, I got a lot to do

SONG

Cat's In The Cradle

ARTIST

Harry Chapin

YEAR

1974

SONGSPIRATION CONTEXT

Chapin once introduced his song at Soundstage like this: "I have some people around me that not only will give me criticism but come up with very strong ideas ... the most important one is my wife. She really came up with many key lines of this song. It's called 'Cats in the Cradle' and it's about my boy Josh. And frankly, the song scares me to death."

FEATURED FONTS

Each created in the year of the song release (from top to bottom, left to right)

URW Scenario

Classified and available through identifont.com

Design: i_dbuero × Carsten Güth

it's a very, very
MAD
WORLD
MAD
WORLD
MAD

SONG
Mad World
ARTIST
Tears for Fears
YEAR
1983

SONGSPIRATION CONTEXT

"'Mad World' hasn't dated because it's expressive of a period I call the teenage menopause, where your hormones are going crazy as you're leaving childhood. Your fingers are on the cliff and you're about to drop off, but somehow you cling on."
(Roland Orzabal, 2013)

FEATURED FONTS

Each created in the year of the song release (from top to bottom, left to right)

Bodoni, Marbrook, Delta Bold

Classified and available through
identifont.com

Design: i_dbuero × Carsten Güth

IT DON'T MATTER IF YOU'RE BLACK OR WHITE

JUNE

SONG
Black Or White
ARTIST
Michael Jackson
YEAR
1991

SONGSPIRATION CONTEXT

The catchy and important message of this song was visualized very impressively in the accompanying music video. With the then brand new “morphing” technique people of all colors and races were morphed into each other. On June 25, 2009, American singer Michael Jackson died of acute propofol and benzodiazepine intoxication at his home on North Carolwood Drive in the Holmby Hills neighborhood of Los Angeles, California.

FEATURED FONTS

Each created in the year of the song release (from top to bottom, left to right)

Advert

Classified and available through identifont.com

Design: i_dbuero × Sabine Schneider

AL
WA
YS
LOOK
AT T
HE B
RIG
HT S
IDE
OF L
IFE

SONG
Always Look At The Bright Side Of Life

ARTIST
Monty Python

YEAR
1989

SONGSPIRATION CONTEXT

British humour rules! When the destroyer *HMS Sheffield* was hit by an Exocet cruise missile during the Falklands War in 1982, the crew sang the song as they waited for their sinking ship to be rescued. Since 2014 this song has become the most popular tune to play at a UK funeral.

FEATURED FONTS

Each created in the year of the song release (from top to bottom, left to right)

Trajan

Classified and available through identifont.com

Design: i_dbuero × OA Krimmel

Gotta
KISS
MYSELF,
I'm so
pretty

SONG
Uptown Funk
ARTIST
Mark Ronson feat. Bruno Mars
YEAR
2015

SONGSPIRATION CONTEXT

The line "gotta kiss myself I'm so pretty" is something that boxing champ Larry Holmes said in an interview where he started talking about how much he loves himself – he then proceeded to kiss his own arms to make his point. Before Holmes, Muhammad Ali often boasted, "I'm so pretty ..." and note that after Bruno Mars says the line, he makes a kissing sound to punctuate it. (songfacts.com)

FEATURED FONTS

Each created in the year of the song release (from top to bottom, left to right)

Modern Love Grunge

Classified and available through identifont.com

Design: i_dbuero × Evelyn Binder

YOU BETTER

LOSE

YOURSELF

IN THE

MUSIC

SONG
Lose Yourself
ARTIST
Eminem
YEAR
2002

SONGSPIRATION CONTEXT

"But music is reflection of self, we just explain it, and then we get our checks in the mail."
(Eminem)

FEATURED FONTS

Each created in the year of the song release (from top to bottom, left to right)

Dokyo

Classified and available through identifont.com

Design: i_dbuero × Carsten Güth

You can't hurry love

SONG
You Can't Hurry Love

ARTIST
The Supremes

YEAR
1966

SONGSPIRATION CONTEXT

Florence Ballard – one of the original founding members of The Supremes – picked the band's name out of a hat in the Motown offices. And the rest is history: The Supremes were the first girl group to be inducted into the Rock and Roll Hall of Fame in 1988.

FEATURED FONTS

Each created in the year of the song release (from top to bottom, left to right)

Annlie

Classified and available through identifont.com

Design: i_dbuero × Ralph Rieker

WAKE UP

AND

LIVE

JUNE

SONG
Wake Up And Live
ARTIST
Bob Marley & The Wailers
YEAR
1979

SONGSPIRATION CONTEXT
One of the weirdest Bob Marley facts out there is that he could apparently read palms as a child. Up until the age of about seven, he would study the palms of friends and neighbours and, remarkably, accurately predict their futures. This unsettled his mother somewhat, but that's not the reason Marley's palm reading was short lived. After returning to his rural village from Kingston, Marley told people that his destiny was to be a singer, and refused to read palms again for the rest of his life.

FEATURED FONTS
Each created in the year of the song release (from top to bottom, left to right)

Milka, ITC Benguiat Gothic, Romic Extra

Classified and available through identifont.com

Design: i_dbuero × Evelyn Binder

YOU WERE

born

TO BE

1

JULY

SONG
Born To Be Alive
ARTIST
Patrick Hernandez
YEAR
1979

SONGSPIRATION CONTEXT

During a stay in New York in 1979, Patrick Hernandez and his producer casted dancers for his world tour, which included the then unknown dancing and singing young lady Ciccone – later world famous as Madonna.

FEATURED FONTS

Each created in the year of the song release (from top to bottom, left to right)

Milka, Accolade

Classified and available through identifont.com

Design: i_dbuero × OA Krimmel

half of the time

and we don't know where

SONG
Only Living Boy in New York
ARTIST
Simon & Garfunkel
YEAR
1970

SONGSPIRATION CONTEXT

The year is half-finished! Is the glass half empty or half full?
You decide ...

FEATURED FONTS

Each created in the year of the song release (from top to bottom, left to right)

ITC Avant Garde, Fools Gold, Jolly Roger Shadow, Hoodoo, Diagonal ND, Data 70, Premier Shaded, Cruz Swinger, Octopuss Shaded

Classified and available through identifont.com

Design: i_dbuero × OA Krimmel

DON'T TELL ME THAT IT'S OVER

IT'S ONLY

JUST

BEGUN

SONG
Don't Tell Me That It's Over
ARTIST
Amy Macdonald
YEAR
2010

SONGSPIRATION CONTEXT

The dog days of summer last from July 3 to August 11. The term 'dog days' traditionally refers to a period of particularly hot and humid weather occurring during the summer months of July and August in the Northern Hemisphere.

"Dog Days bright and clear
Indicate a happy year;
But when accompanied by rain,
For better times, our hopes are vain."

FEATURED FONTS

Each created in the year of the song release (from top to bottom, left to right)

Acier BAT, Text Noir

Classified and available through identifont.com

Design: i_dbuero × Evelyn Binder

What do they make **dreams** for?

SONG
Blurred Lines
ARTIST
Robin Thicke feat. T.I. and Pharrell Williams
YEAR
2013

SONGSPIRATION CONTEXT
Today, the United States of America celebrate its Independence Day (as they do every year). On this day in 1776, the formerly British Thirteen Colonies were first named 'United States of America' in an official document.

FEATURED FONTS
Each created in the year of the song release (from top to bottom, left to right)

Kahlo Rounded Swash, HWT Arabesque

Classified and available through identifont.com

Design: i_dbuero × Evelyn Binder

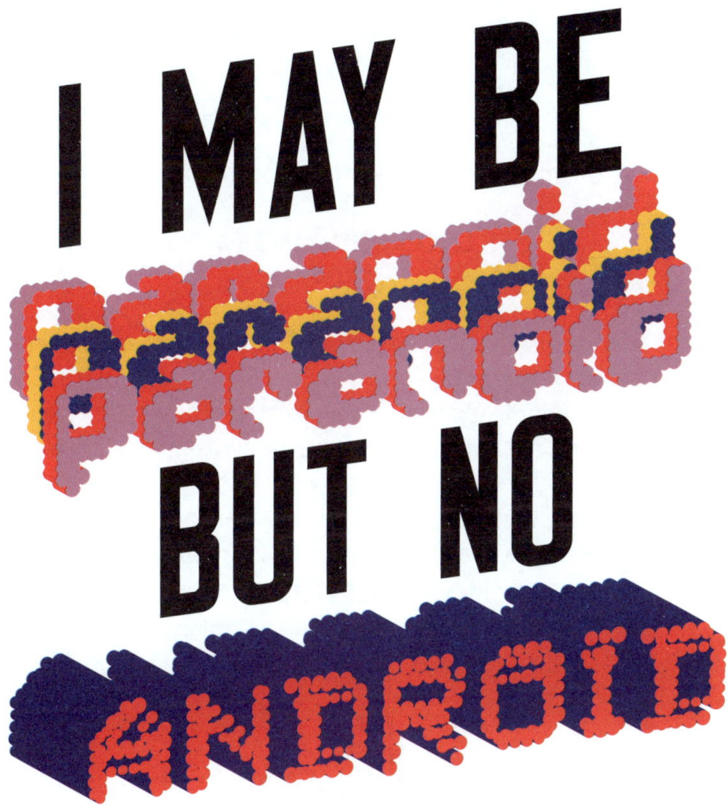
I MAY BE
paranoid
paranoid
paranoid
BUT NO
ANDROID

SONG
Paranoid Android
ARTIST
Radiohead
YEAR
1997

SONGSPIRATION CONTEXT

"It's about being exposed to God, I dunno. It was that one night, really. We'd been rehearsing the song for months, but the lyrics came to me at five o'clock that morning. I was trying to sleep when I literally heard these voices that wouldn't leave me alone. They were the voices of the people I'd heard in the bar. It turned out to be a notorious, coke-fiend place, but I didn't know that. Basically it's just about chaos, chaos, utter f--king chaos." (Lead singer Thom Yorke)

FEATURED FONTS

Each created in the year of the song release (from top to bottom, left to right)

Nomad, Chemo Bubble, Doom Platoon

Classified and available through identifont.com

Design: i_dbuero × Carsten Güth

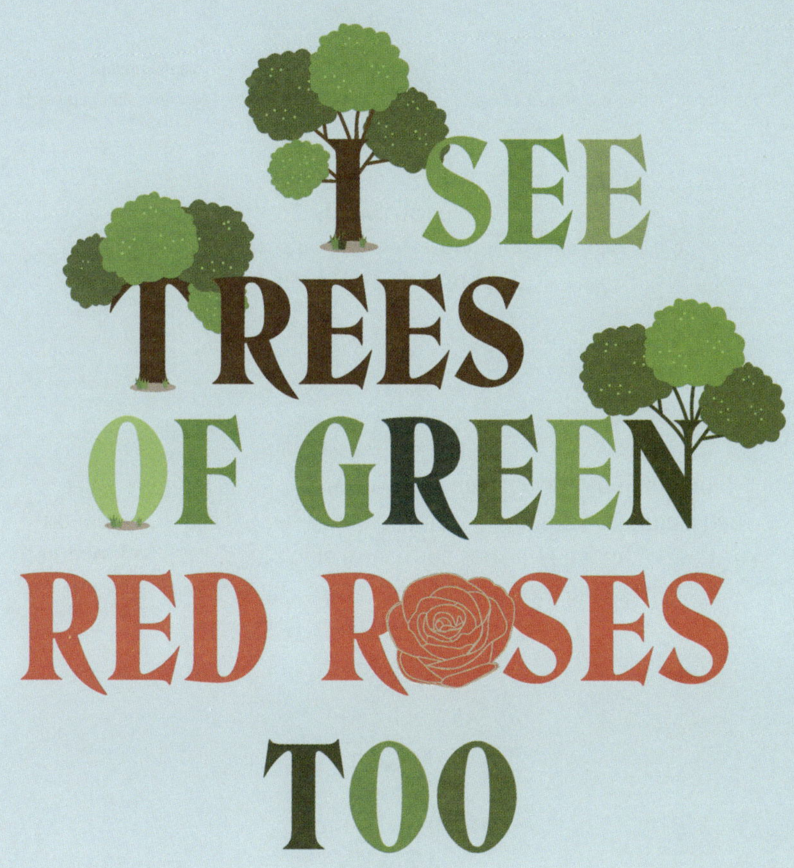
I SEE
TREES
OF GREEN
RED ROSES
TOO

SONG
What a Wonderful World

ARTIST
Louis Armstrong

YEAR
1968

SONGSPIRATION CONTEXT
“It seems to me, it ain’t the world that’s so bad, but what we‘re doing to it”. That’s what Louis Armstrong sang in the intro to the 1970 version of his biggest hit, which he released for the first time when he was still 66 years old. A very wise man, Good Old Satchmo, he died on July 6, 1971.

FEATURED FONTS
Each created in the year of the song release (from top to bottom, left to right)

Hawthorn

Classified and available through identifont.com

Design: i_dbuero × Sabine Schneider

7

JULY

SONG
Ice Cream
ARTIST
Selena Gomez, Black Pink
YEAR
2020

SONGSPIRATION CONTEXT

The origins of ice cream or frozen desserts in general are obscure although several accounts exist about their history. Some sources describe ice cream-like foods as originating in Persia as far back as 550 BC while others claim that the Roman Emperor Nero had ice collected from the Apennine Mountains to produce the first sorbet mixed with honey and wine.

FEATURED FONTS

Each created in the year of the song release (from top to bottom, left to right)

Eastman Grotesque, Apparel Display

Classified and available through identifont.com

Design: i_dbuero × Evelyn Binder

All in all

you're just

another brick

in the wall

SONG
Another Brick in the Wall
ARTIST
Pink Floyd
YEAR
1979

SONGSPIRATION CONTEXT

Few songs in music history have been so readily and lustily misunderstood as 'Another Brick in the Wall'. The piece became the soundtrack of the anarchist protest movement but in the overall context of the album, the three parts of the piece illustrate important stages that lead to the main character piling more and more *bricks* to a *wall* around his soul. In addition to the then merciless British school system, these are, at least equally, the loss of the father, the inability to show emotions, the domineering mother and a failed marriage.

FEATURED FONTS

Each created in the year of the song release (from top to bottom, left to right)

Stratford SH

Classified and available through identifont.com

Design: i_dbuero × Sabine Schneider

TEQUILA!

SONG
Tequila
ARTIST
The Champs
YEAR
1958

SONGSPIRATION CONTEXT

One of the most famous songs in the world – with lyrics consisting of just one singular word! The songwriter Danny Flores is the singer and also the saxophonist. Tequila, the liquor itself, by the way, is made from the blue agave, which grows mainly in the area around the Mexican city of Tequila. Just like the song, the agave spirit is a veritable hit – a golden oldie.

FEATURED FONTS

Each created in the year of the song release (from top to bottom, left to right)

Recta

Classified and available through identifont.com

Design: i_dbuero × Carsten Güth

Don't
let
your

pass
you
by

life
life
life
life
life
life
life
life
life
life
life

SONG
I Will Remember You

ARTIST
Sarah McLachlan

YEAR
1993

SONGSPIRATION CONTEXT

"You only live once,
but if you do it right,
once is enough."
(Mae West)

FEATURED FONTS

Each created in the year of the song release (from top to bottom, left to right)

Interstate

Classified and available through
identifont.com

Design: i_dbuero × Carsten Güth

GOOD
LIFE
GOOD
LIFE
GOOD
LIFE
GOOD
LIFE
GOOD
LIFE

Just
don't
let
the

pass
you
by

SONG
Don’t Let The Good Life Pass You By
ARTIST
Cass Elliot
YEAR
1973

SONGSPIRATION CONTEXT

“There are three ingredients in the good life:
learning, earning and yearning.”
(Christopher Morley)

FEATURED FONTS

Each created in the year of the song release (from top to bottom, left to right)

Maximus, Shatter

Classified and available through identifont.com

Design: i_dbuero × Carsten Güth

KISSING
SEXING
CASIO
POKE

I

12

JULY

SONG
Over And Over
ARTIST
Hot Chip
YEAR
2006

SONGSPIRATION CONTEXT

The joy of repetition really is in you: Hot Chip's Alexis Taylor told Mojo magazine that the song was written, "when I was interested in hypnotic, repetitive music like Terry Riley's *A Rainbow in Curved Air.* If you get a good loop going, you could listen to it forever. You hear something different every repeat."

FEATURED FONTS

Each created in the year of the song release (from top to bottom, left to right)

Flat 10

Classified and available through
identifont.com

Design: i_dbuero × Carsten Güth

BUT IT'S NOT
FOREVER

BUT IT'S JUST
TONIGHT

SONG
Sex on Fire
ARTIST
Kings of Leon
YEAR
2008

SONGSPIRATION CONTEXT

From blackout to baby boom in just 9 months: the New York City Blackout happened on July 13, 1977. The blackout lasted 25 hours in some neighbourhoods. Nine months later, hospitals there reported birth rates up to 3 times higher than usual.

FEATURED FONTS

Each created in the year of the song release (from top to bottom, left to right)

Hedgerow, Shelton

Classified and available through identifont.com

Design: i_dbuero × Carsten Güth

Tomorrow

SONG
Ruby
ARTIST
Kaiser Chiefs
YEAR
2007

SONGSPIRATION CONTEXT

14 July is the French national holiday. They celebrate the 'national reconciliation' of France on this day. *Liberté, Égalité, Fraternité*: With this battle cry, militias from the Paris districts stormed Louis XVI's state prison in eastern Paris on 14 July 1789. This battle cry became famous and has been firmly anchored in the social memory of the French and in history books ever since. This day marks the beginning of the French Revolution.

FEATURED FONTS

Each created in the year of the song release (from top to bottom, left to right)

Guillotine

Classified and available through
identifont.com

Design: i_dbuero × OA Krimmel
Celebrating: Ruby Carla Jo

TO
MOR
ROW'S
JUST ANOTHER
DAY

SONG
Tomorrow's Just Another Day
ARTIST
Madness
YEAR
1983

SONGSPIRATION CONTEXT

"The extreme limit of wisdom,
that's what the public calls madness."
(Jean Cocteau)

FEATURED FONTS

Each created in the year of the song release (from top to bottom, left to right)

Chicago (meets Krungthep)

Classified and available through identifont.com

Design: i_dbuero × OA Krimmel

DON'T YOU
KNOW THAT
YOU'RE
TOXIC?

SONG
Toxic
ARTIST
Britney Spears
YEAR
2004

SONGSPIRATION CONTEXT

"If you walked away from a toxic, negative, abusive, one-sided, dead-end, low vibrational relationship or friendship – you won." (Lalah Delia)

FEATURED FONTS

Each created in the year of the song release (from top to bottom, left to right)

State Machine

Classified and available through identifont.com

Design: i_dbuero × Evelyn Binder

NOW
YOU'RE
GIVING
ME THE
LOOK
LOOK

SONG
The Look
ARTIST
Metronomy
YEAR
2010

SONGSPIRATION CONTEXT

Today is World Emoji Day. Since 2013, the website Emojipedia.com has documented all Unicode emojis with names, descriptions and images. Choose 'The Look' for you there.

FEATURED FONTS

Each created in the year of the song release (from top to bottom, left to right)

Hunk

Classified and available through identifont.com

Design: i_dbuero × Carsten Güth

FREE YOUR MIND

... YOUR ASS

WILL FOLLOW

SONG
Free Your Mind

ARTIST
Funkadelic

YEAR
1970

SONGSPIRATION CONTEXT
In a Songfacts interview George Clinton said he was tripping on acid when he came up with the title phrase. "I didn't even know that I had said it to one of the guys that was working with us. He said, 'You said something really deep, and the people liked it.' And you will like hearing that song through your earphones to get funkadelic.

FEATURED FONTS
Each created in the year of the song release (from top to bottom, left to right)

Jolly Roger

Classified and available through identifont.com

Design: i_dbuero × Syl Hillier

LONELY
DAYS ARE GONE,
I'M A-GOIN' HOME

09 07 00 47

WIEN SCHWECHAT
F 004

AIRMAIL

My Baby,
just wrote
me a letter

XX

SONG
The Letter
ARTIST
The Box Tops
YEAR
1967

SONGSPIRATION CONTEXT

When the group recorded this, they still did not have a name. One band member suggested, "Let's have a contest and everybody can send in 50 cents and a box top." Producer Dan Penn then dubbed them The Box Tops. (songfacts.com)

FEATURED FONTS

Each created in the year of the song release (from top to bottom, left to right)

Press Gothic, Nevison Casual

Classified and available through identifont.com

Design: i_dbuero × Carsten Güth

how wonderful life is while you're in the world

20

JULY

SONG
Your Song
ARTIST
Elton John
YEAR
1971

SONGSPIRATION CONTEXT

"The more removed you become from the person you're naturally supposed to be – the harder you're making your life and the less happy you become." (Elton John)

FEATURED FONTS

Each created in the year of the song release (from top to bottom, left to right)

Spadina

Classified and available through identifont.com

Design: i_dbuero × Sabine Schneider

walking on the

MOON

SONG
Walking On The Moon
ARTIST
The Police
YEAR
1979

SONGSPIRATION CONTEXT

On July 21, 1969, over a billion people watched the first man walking on the moon. And listened to his famous quote: “That’s one small step for man, one giant leap for mankind.” It went on to inspire The Police to write this song 10 years later.

FEATURED FONTS

Each created in the year of the song release (from top to bottom, left to right)

Harlow Solid, Milka Aged

Classified and available through identifont.com

Design: i_dbuero × Evelyn Binder

I CAN'T TELL
YOU WHAT
IT REALLY IS
I CAN ONLY
TELL YOU
WHAT
IT FEELS LIKE

SONG
Love the Way you lie
ARTIST
Eminem & Rihanna
YEAR
2010

SONGSPIRATION CONTEXT

Today is Pi Day.
Why today exactly?
Of course, a bit of mathematics is part of the solution to the riddle.

Any ideas?!
Because 22/7 comes pretty close to the number Pi ...

FEATURED FONTS

Each created in the year of the song release (from top to bottom, left to right)

Vow, Acier BAT Text Noir

Classified and available through identifont.com

Design: i_dbuero × Evelyn Binder

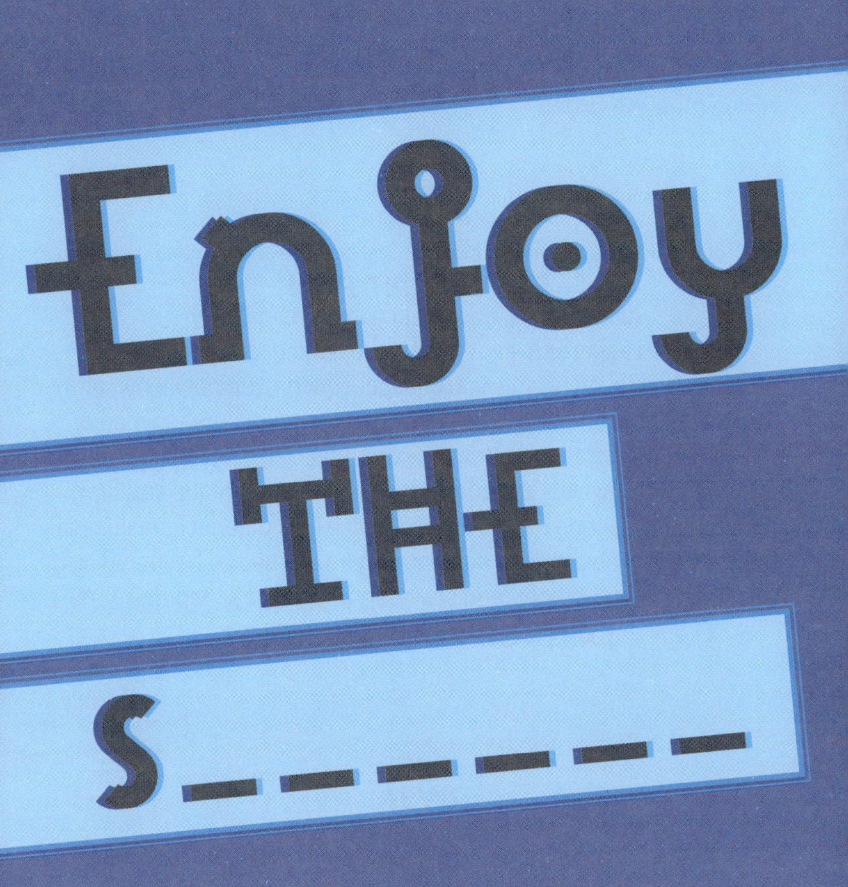
Enjoy
THE
S_ _ _ _ _ _

SONG
Enjoy the Silence
ARTIST
Depeche Mode
YEAR
1990

SONGSPIRATION CONTEXT

Happy birthday, Martin Gore! Gore was born today in 1961. When Flood [the producer] turned Martin Gore's demo song, which was a slow ballad and orchestrated with a harmonium, into an upbeat disco number, Gore was not amused at all in the beginning: "This is not my kind of disco". Reluctantly, he contributed the appropriate guitar riff and went to bed. But after another day of mixing, the band quickly agreed, as Gore later recounts: "I think that's the only time in our history when we all looked at each other and said, 'I think this might be a hit.'" And it became one of their biggest hits ever.

FEATURED FONTS

Each created in the year of the song release (from top to bottom, left to right)

Cattlebrand

Classified and available through identifont.com

Design: i_dbuero × OA Krimmel

IT'S SOMETHING MAGICAL
IT'S IN THE AIR,
IT'S IN MY BLOOD,
IT'S RUSHING ON

SONG
Can't Stop the Feeling
ARTIST
Justin Timberlake
YEAR
2016

SONGSPIRATION CONTEXT

Justin Timberlake once left some of his half-eaten French toast in a restaurant, and the waiter sold it on eBay for $1,025!

FEATURED FONTS

Each created in the year of the song release (from top to bottom, left to right)

Hobeaux Rococeaux

Classified and available through identifont.com

Design: i_dbuero × Evelyn Binder

Aha,
aha,
AHA.

SONG
Da Da Da
ARTIST
Trio
YEAR
1981

SONGSPIRATION CONTEXT

Trio guitarist Kralle Krawinkel moved to Spain a few years after their great successes. From there he made it into the *Guinness Book of Records* in 1998. He rode a horse from Seville across Europe to Hamburg – the longest horseback trek up to that point. Today is National Day of the Cowboy!

FEATURED FONTS

Each created in the year of the song release (from top to bottom, left to right)

Motter Femina, Princetown, Barcelona

Classified and available through identifont.com

Design: i_dbuero × OA Krimmel

IF WE WEREN'T ALL

CRAZY

WE WOULD GO

INSANE

26

JULY

SONG

Changes in Latitudes, Changes in Attitudes

ARTIST

Jimmy Buffett

YEAR

1977

SONGSPIRATION CONTEXT

"Dreaming permits each and every one of us to be quietly and safely insane every night of the week."
(William Dement)

FEATURED FONTS

Each created in the year of the song release (from top to bottom, left to right)

Praxis, Cortez, ITC Benguiat Gothic, Thornface Sharp, Souvenir Gothic, Chesterfield

Classified and available through identifont.com

Design: i_dbuero × Evelyn Binder

Go and dance yourself clean, yeah

SONG
Dance Yrself Clean

ARTIST
LCD Soundsystem

YEAR
2010

SONGSPIRATION CONTEXT
Today is officially Take Your Houseplants for a Walk Day.
Have a try – it works even better if you are doing it dancing.

FEATURED FONTS
Each created in the year of the song release (from top to bottom, left to right)

Reklame Script

Classified and available through identifont.com

Design: i_dbuero × Carsten Güth

WORK IT, MAKE IT, DO IT

JULY

SONG
Harder, Better, Faster, Stronger
ARTIST
Daft Punk
YEAR
2001

SONGSPIRATION CONTEXT

Au revoir Daft Punk. *Harder, better, faster* and *stronger* was also the French duo's official break-up in 2021. An eight-minute video on YouTube, called 'Epilogue': one is blown up, the other walks into the sunset. The end. After 25 years, the Hit Robots no longer produce hits; but they have left behind a rich legacy: 'Get Lucky', 'One More Time', 'Around the World' and umpteen other dance anthems. Merci beaucoup.

FEATURED FONTS

Each created in the year of the song release (from top to bottom, left to right)

Mostra Nuova

Classified and available through identifont.com

Design: i_dbuero × Tim Oliver Schweizer

So tell me
what
you want,
what you
really,
really want

29

JULY

SONG
Wannabe
ARTIST
Spice Girls
YEAR
1996

SONGSPIRATION CONTEXT

"Being in the Spice Girls was an insane experience."
(Melanie Chisholm)

FEATURED FONTS

Each created in the year of the song release (from top to bottom, left to right)

ITC Klepto

Classified and available through identifont.com

Design: i_dbuero × Carsten Güth

ALLES
NUR
SHOW

WIR TUN ALLE
NUR SO

SONG
Show
ARTIST
Thomas D & The KBCS
YEAR
2021

SONGSPIRATION CONTEXT

"Happy release day to myself" tweeted Thomas D on 30 July 2021. His new single 'Show' was out. All just for show? Not at all, Thomas D has a lot of clever thoughts and learned life lessons behind it. This song shows it.

FEATURED FONTS

Each created in the year of the song release (from top to bottom, left to right)

GT America

Classified and available through identifont.com

Design: i_dbuero × Sabine Schneider

YOU CAN CHECK OUT ANY TIME YOU LIKE*

*BUT YOU CAN NEVER LEAVE

SONG
Hotel California
ARTIST
Eagles
YEAR
1976

SONGSPIRATION CONTEXT

"On just about every album we made, there was some kind of commentary on the music business, and on American culture in general. The hotel itself could be taken as a metaphor not only for the myth-making of Southern California, but for the myth-making that is the American Dream, because it is a fine line between the American Dream, and the American nightmare."
(Singer Don Henley)

FEATURED FONTS

Each created in the year of the song release (from top to bottom, left to right)

Agenda Bg

Classified and available through identifont.com

Design: i_dbuero × Sabine Schneider

Take A Walk

ON THE WILD SIDE

AUGUST

SONG
Walk on the Wild Side
ARTIST
Lou Reed
YEAR
1972

SONGSPIRATION CONTEXT

On 1 August 1936, the Olympic Games opened in Berlin. African American Jesse Owen initially did not want to compete in a racist country, but eventually did and became the most successful athlete of the Olympics with four gold medals in running and the long jump. So finally, in the middle of Nazi Germany, a black athlete was frenetically celebrated.

FEATURED FONTS

Each created in the year of the song release (from top to bottom, left to right)

Lazybones, Serpentine Bold

Classified and available through
identifont.com

Design: i_dbuero × OA Krimmel

Soll ich's wirklich machen

oder lass ich's lieber sein?

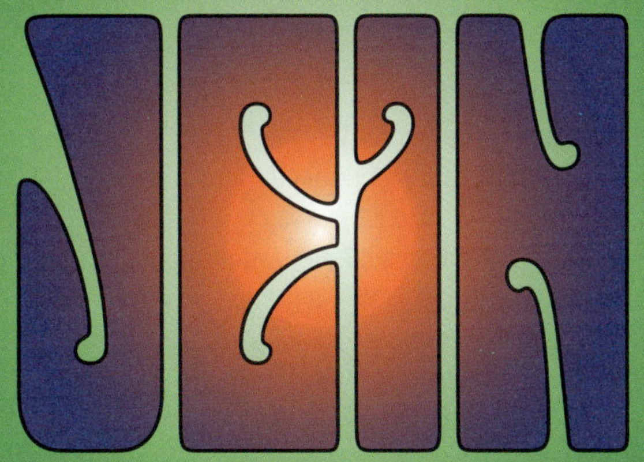

2

AUGUST

SONG
Jein
ARTIST
Fettes Brot
YEAR
1996

SONGSPIRATION CONTEXT

A portmanteau word, like 'Jein' (from Ja and Nein – Yes and No), is a word that has arisen from at least two morphologically overlapping words that have merged to form a new concept in terms of content. The underlying word-formation process is referred to as amalgamation, contamination, terminology crossover, word blending, [word] fusion or word entanglement. A well-known example is brunch (from breakfast and lunch). Typically, contamination is conceptually motivated and the words involved belong to one word class. (wikipedia)

FEATURED FONTS

Each created in the year of the song release (from top to bottom, left to right)

Chalet 1970, Mojo

Classified and available through identifont.com

Design: i_dbuero × Thomas Hofmann

Isolation
is not
good
for me
Isolation I don't want to sit on a

Lemon
tree

SONG
Lemon Tree
ARTIST
Fool's Garden
YEAR
1995

SONGSPIRATION RELATION

On this day in 1492, Christopher Columbus set sail from Palos, Spain, with three ships, *Nina*, *Pinta* and *Santa Maria*. He discovered new worlds and food. But he also brought something with him, among other things, the lemon tree. It was Columbus who paved the way for the lemon tree across the Atlantic Ocean. Since then, there has been no stopping the exotic lemon tree. Today, the largest cultivation areas exist in Spain, Mexico, India and Argentina.

FEATURED FONTS

Each created in the year of the song release (from top to bottom, left to right)

FF Magda Pro, Mardi Gras

Classified and available through identifont.com

Design: i_dbuero × Kristin Munz

IT'S ALL

TOO

beautiful

4

AUGUST

SONG
Itchycoo Park
ARTIST
Small Faces
YEAR
1967

SONGSPIRATION CONTEXT

The songwriter Steve Marriott stated that 'Itchycoo Park' is Valentine's Park in Ilford. 'We used to go there and get stung by wasps. It's what we used to call it'. This song was released on 4 August 1967.

FEATURED FONTS

Each created in the year of the song release (from top to bottom, left to right)

Neil, Snell Roundhand

Classified and available through identifont.com

Design: i_dbuero × Carsten Güth

5

AUGUST

SONG
Closing Time
ARTIST
Semisonic
YEAR
1998

SONGSPIRATION CONTEXT

On this day in 1962, the film star Marilyn Monroe died at age 36 from an overdose of sleeping pills. She left her mark on Hollywood and the film industry like no other star before or after her. Her example and her tragic career have influenced many new generations since.

FEATURED FONTS

Each created in the year of the song release (from top to bottom, left to right)

Alpha Niner

Classified and available through identifont.com

Design: i_dbuero × Sabine Schneider

I GOT A
HOT SAUCE
IN MY BAG,
SWAG

SONG
Formation
ARTIST
Beyoncé
YEAR
2016

SONGSPIRATION CONTEXT

On August 6, 1762, the first-ever sandwich was created, at least with such a name. It was named after the Earl of Sandwich when he requested a dish involving meat between two pieces of bread. As the story goes, he requested it as he was in the middle of a gambling game and didn't want to interrupt it. (#thefactside)

FEATURED FONTS

Each created in the year of the song release (from top to bottom, left to right)

DK Antidote

Classified and available through identifont.com

Design: i_dbuero × Evelyn Binder

Good mornin' life
Good mornin' world,

how are you happiness 

SONG
Good Mornin' Life

ARTIST
Dean Martin

YEAR
1957

SONGSPIRATION CONTEXT
Today was a fun date back in 1990:
At 12:34:56 the time and date was 12:34:56 7/8/90,
i.e. 1234567890.

FEATURED FONTS
Each created in the year of the song release (from top to bottom, left to right)

Neue Haas Grotesk

Classified and available through
identifont.com

Design: i_dbuero × Carsten Güth

we bite and
scratch
and scream
all night

SONG
The Lovecats
ARTIST
The Cure
YEAR
1983

SONGSPIRATION CONTEXT

It's International Cat Day. #catcontent: 'A study has found that viewing not-yet-adult cats, which are considered cute, can increase productivity and actions are taken more carefully after viewing such photos.' (The Power of Kawaii)

FEATURED FONTS

Each created in the year of the song release (from top to bottom, left to right)

Agincourt, Santa Fe

Classified and available through identifont.com

Design: i_dbuero × Katrin Schlüsener

9

AUGUST

SONG
The Power
ARTIST
Snap!
YEAR
1990

SONGSPIRATION CONTEXT

Most of the power in SONGSPIRATION comes from the music, of course. But right after that come the typefaces. The typefaces have the power to present every message in a very individual and emotional form. Fonts are, next to photos and icons, the most important content conveyors in the world. They've got the power! Many thanks to all the font designers, without whose great work this calendar would not be possible.

FEATURED FONTS

Each created in the year of the song release (from top to bottom, left to right)

Strobos

Classified and available through
identifont.com

Design: i_dbuero × OA Krimmel
Celebrating Dana Wyse

dying
is easy
it's
living
that
scares me
to death

10 AUGUST

SONG
Cold
ARTIST
Annie Lennox
YEAR
2017

SONGSPIRATION CONTEXT

On this day in 2005, a 28-year-old South Korean man played the video game *Starcraft* for 49 hours straight – and then died of exhaustion.

FEATURED FONTS

Each created in the year of the song release (from top to bottom, left to right)

Garnett

Classified and available through identifont.com

Design: i_dbuero × Sabine Schneider

WHAT THE HELL

AM I DOING HERE?

SONG
Creep
ARTIST
Radiohead
YEAR
1992

SONGSPIRATION CONTEXT

"I have a real problem being a man in the '90s … Any man with any sensitivity or conscience toward the opposite sex would have a prob-lem. To actually assert yourself in a masculine way without looking like you're in a hard-rock band is a very difficult thing to do … It comes back to the music we write, which is not effeminate, but it's not brutal in its arrogance. It is one of the things I'm always trying: To assert a sexual persona and on the other hand trying desperately to negate it." (lead singer Thom Yorke about the song)

FEATURED FONTS

Each created in the year of the song release (from top to bottom, left to right)

Phosphate

Classified and available through identifont.com

Design: i_dbuero × Jochen Schieborn

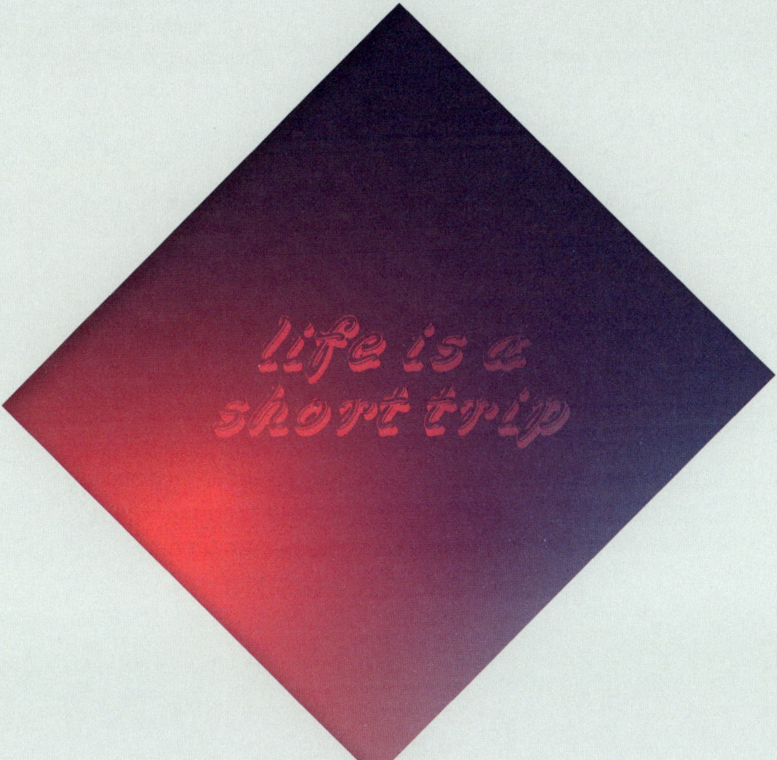

life is a
short trip

AUGUST

SONG
Forever Young
ARTIST
Alphaville
YEAR
1984

SONGSPIRATION CONTEXT

Today we celebrate International Youth Day.
“Youth is happy because it has the capacity to see beauty.
Anyone who keeps the ability to see beauty never grows old.”
(Franz Kafka)

FEATURED FONTS

Each created in the year of the song release (from top to bottom, left to right)
Vegas

Classified and available through identifont.com

Design: i_dbuero × Hannah Hoffmann

F ck
'em

SONG
Fuck Em
ARTIST
T.I.
YEAR
2021

SONGSPIRATION CONTEXT

In the early hours of 13 August 1961, GDR security forces sealed off the sector border in Berlin. Barricades were erected, concrete posts driven into the ground and barbed wire fences drawn. The passage from East to West was blocked, the city divided into two halves. The Berlin Wall separated East and West for more than 28 years. It became a symbol of the conflict-ridden post-war order.

FEATURED FONTS

Each created in the year of the song release (from top to bottom, left to right)

Yink

Classified and available through identifont.com

Design: i_dbuero × OA Krimmel

I'M SPINNING
AROUND
MOVE OUTTA
MY WAY

SONG
Spinning Around
ARTIST
Kylie Minogue
YEAR
2000

SONGSPIRATION CONTEXT

This was co-written by Paula Abdul, who was going to record it for her comeback. She decided to give the whole thing a miss and revived her career by becoming a judge on the TV show A*merican Idol*. Kylie got the song and became the comeback queen. (songfacts.com)

FEATURED FONTS

Each created in the year of the song release (from top to bottom, left to right)

Dimitri Regular, Dimitri Swank

Classified and available through identifont.com

Design: i_dbuero × Evelyn Binder

LET
THE SUN
BEAT DOWN
UPON MY FACE

AND
STARS
FILL MY
DREAM

SONG
Kashmir
ARTIST
Led Zeppelin
YEAR
1975

SONGSPIRATION CONTEXT

On this day in 1969, the legendary Woodstock Festival began. Led Zeppelin had preferred the beach to the mud of Woodstock that summer, and on this weekend they played in Ashbury Park on the Atlantic coast of New Jersey. Peter Grant, Led Zeppelin's manager at the time, is quoted in the book *Led Zeppelin: the Concert File* as saying: „I said no to Woodstock because we would have been just another band on the bill there." They were very angry about this decision for quite a while.

FEATURED FONTS

Each created in the year of the song release (from top to bottom, left to right)

Fehrle

Classified and available through identifont.com

Design: i_dbuero × Sabine Schneider

ALL I'M ASKIN' IS FOR A LITTLE RESPECT

AUGUST

SONG
Respect
ARTIST
Aretha Franklin
YEAR
1967

SONGSPIRATION CONTEXT

Aretha Franklin died of pancreatic cancer on 16 August 2018 at the age of 76. Before her funeral, the soul legend laid in state for two days in a gleaming gold coffin at the Wright Museum of African American History in Michigan to give her fans, who queued in long lines for two days, the opportunity to pay their last respects (!).

FEATURED FONTS

Each created in the year of the song release (from top to bottom, left to right)

Press Gothic

Classified and available through identifont.com

Design: i_dbuero × Caroline Glock

There is a crack,
a crack in everything

That's how
the light
gets in

17

AUGUST

SONG
Anthem
ARTIST
Leonard Cohen
YEAR
1992

SONGSPIRATION CONTEXT

Bill Clinton was the first sitting president to testify before a grand jury. On 17 August 1998, he appeared on national television and gave his speech, admitting to having had an inappropriate relationship with former White House intern Monica Lewinsky. His admission came several months after a much-publicised denial.

FEATURED FONTS

Each created in the year of the song release (from top to bottom, left to right)

Interpol

Classified and available through
identifont.com

Design: i_dbuero × Carsten Güth

AND I DON'T
WANT A
NEVER-ENDING
LIFE
I JUST WANT
to be alive
WHILE
I'M HERE

SONG
Spirits
ARTIST
The Strumbellas
YEAR
2016

SONGSPIRATION CONTEXT

“I started struggling with depression when I was 18 and managing it has been extraordinarily hard. Some days are a lot harder than others,” lead vocalist Simon Ward explained. “I’ve always found picking up my guitar helps. I’ve always used creating music as an emotional outlet. [...] It’s not always easy, but I talk about my struggles in my songs because I know what it’s like to feel alone and if my music can give even one other person hope, then that’s all that matters to me.”

FEATURED FONTS

Each created in the year of the song release (from top to bottom, left to right)

SDK Cinnabar Brush, Chronic, DiMare

Classified and available through identifont.com

Design: i_dbuero × Evelyn Binder

It's gonna be
a bright,
bright
bright
bright
sunshiny
day

19

AUGUST

SONG
I Can See Clearly Now
ARTIST
Johnny Nash
YEAR
1972

SONGSPIRATION CONTEXT

Happy birthday to Johnny Nash, who was born on this day in 1940. He found his groove in Jamaica and recorded his biggest hits 'I Can See Clearly Now' and 'Stir It Up' with the reggae influence he picked up from local musicians like Bob Marley. Nash signed Marley and his group, The Wailers, but Marley would have his first taste of success outside of Jamaica when Nash included a cover of Marley's *Stir It Up* on his own 1972 album *I Can See Clearly Now*.

FEATURED FONTS

Each created in the year of the song release (from top to bottom, left to right)

Aachen

Classified and available through identifont.com

Design: i_dbuero × Anja Osterwalder

wir
sind
die

r o
b o
t e r

20

AUGUST

SONG
Die Roboter
ARTIST
Kraftwerk
YEAR
1978

SONGSPIRATION CONTEXT

One of Kraftwerk's most distinctive signature sounds comes from a Detroit-based device called the Vortrax', which was used in the early '70s to treat deaf-mute children. The device, which is only the size of a pocket calculator, is responsible for the alienated choral vocals heard on 'Uranium'. Today is co-founder Ralf Hütter's birthday (born in 1946).

FEATURED FONTS

Each created in the year of the song release (from top to bottom, left to right)

Milka

Classified and available through identifont.com

Design: i_dbuero × OA Krimmel

— I told you, homeboy

you can't touch this!

AUGUST

SONG
U Can't Touch This

ARTIST
MC Hammer

YEAR
1990

SONGSPIRATION CONTEXT

On 21 August 1911, the Mona Lisa was stolen from the Louvre. The police investigated in all directions, even Pablo Picasso was questioned. It took two years, then the thief, an Italian craftsman, tried to sell the painting and got caught. The painting was well known before, but since then it has become world famous.

FEATURED FONTS

Each created in the year of the song release (from top to bottom, left to right)

Arial

Classified and available through identifont.com

Design: i_dbuero × Martin Drozmann

22

AUGUST

SONG
Bury A Friend
ARTIST
Billie Eilish
YEAR
2019

SONGSPIRATION CONTEXT

On this day in the year 565, the Loch Ness Monster is sighted for the first time. Somehow monsters are just everywhere. At least in our imagination – or under the bed, as in this song by Billie Eilish.

FEATURED FONTS

Each created in the year of the song release (from top to bottom, left to right)

Obviously

Classified and available through identifont.com

Design: i_dbuero × Evelyn Binder

23

AUGUST

SONG
Your Move
ARTIST
Yes
YEAR
1971

SONGSPIRATION CONTEXT

Rick Wakeman has left and rejoined Yes six times. He told *Kerrang!*: "Somebody once said Yes and myself were like Richard Burton and Elizabeth Taylor: couldn't live with each other, but couldn't live without each other. And I said, 'That's absolutely fine – as long as I'm Richard Burton.'"

FEATURED FONTS

Each created in the year of the song release (from top to bottom, left to right)

Spadina

Classified and available through identifont.com

Design: i_dbuero × Sabine Schneider

24

AUGUST

SONG
One More Time
ARTIST
Daft Punk
YEAR
2000

SONGSPIRATION CONTEXT

'We liked similar films and records and then formed a small rock band. Our name was first "Darlin" – named after a song by the Beach Boys. In 1991 we released a few songs on the label of the band Stereolab. And there was a bad review in the London magazine *Melody Maker*. We sounded like "daft punk" – like „stupid punk". We took note of that. When we changed our sound – away from rocknroll and towards the machines - we remembered the criticism and called ourselves "Daft Punk".' (Zündfunk interview in 1997)

FEATURED FONTS

Each created in the year of the song release (from top to bottom, left to right)

Bouchon

Classified and available through identifont.com

Design: i_dbuero × Carsten Güth

Dust yourself off

and try again

SONG
Try Again
ARTIST
Aaliyah
YEAR
2000

SONGSPIRATION CONTEXT

On August 25, 2001, Aaliyah died tragically at the age of 22 in an airplane accident in the Bahamas. Even in the decades since her death, Aaliyah's music has continued to achieve huge success, also by several posthumous releases, and she has sold over 35 million albums worldwide.

FEATURED FONTS

Each created in the year of the song release (from top to bottom, left to right)

Django, Bickham Script

Classified and available through identifont.com

Design: i_dbuero × Katrin Schlüsener

NO
COLORS
ANYMORE
I WANT THEM
TO TURN
BLACK

AUGUST

SONG
Paint It Black
ARTIST
The Rolling Stones
YEAR
1966

SONGSPIRATION CONTEXT

Also a kind of a black story: Brian Jones was a founding member of the Rolling Stones and key to their early success. He was still going strong when this song was released, but fell off the wagon a year later when his drug use caught up to him and his girlfriend, Anita Pallenberg, left him for Keith Richards. By June 1969, he was a liability, and the Stones fired him. Less than a month later he drowned under very mysterious circumstances in his swimming pool at age 27.

FEATURED FONTS

Each created in the year of the song release (from top to bottom, left to right)

Harry Thin Squeezed

Classified and available through identifont.com

Design: i_dbuero × Martin Drozmann

ARE WE

HU MAN

or

ARE WE

DAN CER?

SONG
Human
ARTIST
The Killers
YEAR
2008

SONGSPIRATION CONTEXT

Many of The Killers fans have been mystified why the song's chorus ("Are we human/ Or are we dancer?"), refers to „dancer“ in the singular. MTV News asked singer Brandon Flowers about the nonsensical chorus. He replied: "It's taken from a quote by [author Hunter S.] Thompson: *We're raising a generation of dancers, and I took it and ran. I guess it bothers people that it*'s not grammatically correct, but I think I'm allowed to do whatever I want."

FEATURED FONTS

Each created in the year of the song release (from top to bottom, left to right)

Lalibela

Classified and available through identifont.com

Design: i_dbuero × Mavi Schuler

HANDS UP
REACH FOR THE STARS

HANDS UP
GET'EM UP HIGH

HANDS UP
IF YOU REALLY FEEL ALIVE

SONG
Reach For The Stars

ARTIST
Will.I.Am

YEAR
2012

SONGSPIRATION CONTEXT

This song had travelled 56 million kilometres before the public heard it here on Earth for the first time! NASA itself acted as radio station and beamed the song from Mars to Earth on 28.8.2012. It was the first song ever played from another planet.

FEATURED FONTS

Each created in the year of the song release (from top to bottom, left to right)

Dude, Roboto

Classified and available through identifont.com

Design: i_dbuero × Carsten Güth

10% luck, 20% skill, 15% concentrated power of will, 5% pleasure, 50% pain

SONG
Remember the Name

ARTIST
Fort Minor

YEAR
2005

SONGSPIRATION CONTEXT
"Pain is inevitable, suffering is optional."
(Buddhist proverb)

FEATURED FONTS
Each created in the year of the song release (from top to bottom, left to right)

Avebury

Classified and available through
identifont.com

Design: i_dbuero × OA Krimmel

people
are
strange
when you're a
stranger

30

AUGUST

SONG

People Are Strange

ARTIST

The Doors

YEAR

1967

SONGSPIRATION CONTEXT

Mary Shelley's *Frankenstein* is the second great archetype of the modern horror genre alongside Bram Stoker's *Dracula*. Her novel is about an artificially created human being who, through the cruelty and ignorance of his environment, becomes the monster everyone thinks he is. Really monstrous, on the other hand, are the quite normal people: with their cold hearts and their delusion of having the world under control. Mary Shelley was born on this day in 1797.

FEATURED FONTS

Each created in the year of the song release (from top to bottom, left to right)

Serifa

Classified and available through identifont.com

Design: i_dbuero × Sabine Schneider

AUGUST

SONG
Rolling In The Deep
ARTIST
Adele
YEAR
2010

SONGSPIRATION CONTEXT

Adele had to cancel her concert tour planned for early 2022. The illness of half the crew with COVID-19 and delivery problems forced her to take this step. Deeply moved and in tears, Adele canceled the tour at the last minute on her Instagram channel. But millions of fans understood and sent her endless likes and prayers for her stamina – without the tour having taken place, she still almost *had it all* – at least the applause and the fan love.

FEATURED FONTS

Each created in the year of the song release (from top to bottom, left to right)

Faber Sans

Classified and available through identifont.com

Design: i_dbuero × Carsten Güth

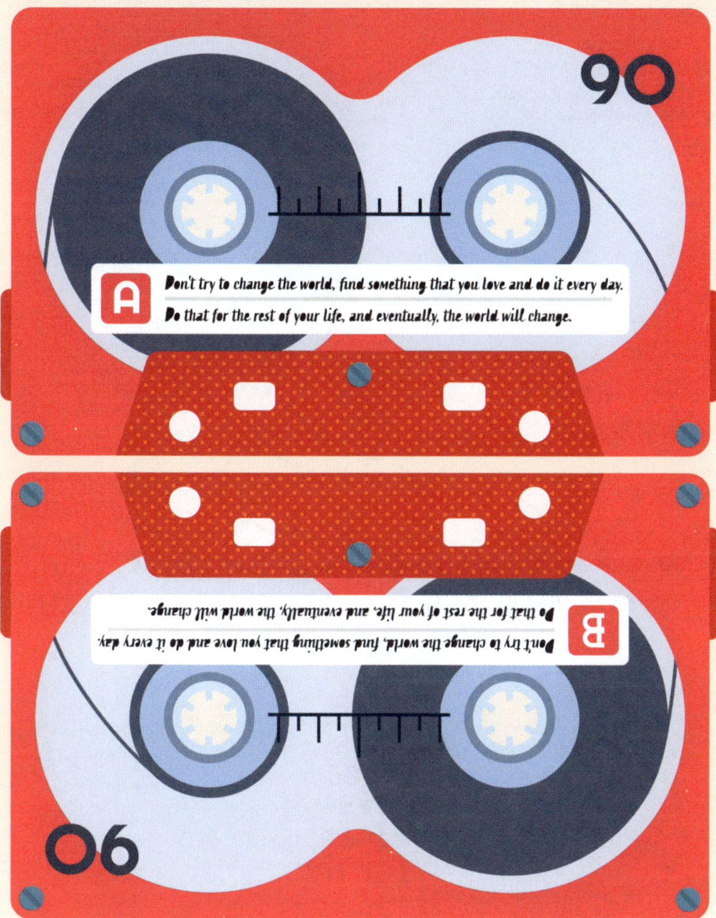

90
A
Don't try to change the world, find something that you love and do it every day.
Do that for the rest of your life, and eventually, the world will change.
B

1

SEPTEMBER

SONG
Growing Up
ARTIST
Macklemore and Ryan Lewis feat. Ed Sheeran
YEAR
2016

SONGSPIRATION CONTEXT

From a meteorological point of view, 1 September is the beginning of autumn in the northern hemisphere and the beginning of spring in the southern hemisphere.

FEATURED FONTS

Each created in the year of the song release (from top to bottom, left to right)

Active

Classified and available through identifont.com

Design: i_dbuero × OA Krimmel

2

SEPTEMBER

SONG
Can’t Take My Eyes Off You

ARTIST
Frankie Valli

YEAR
1967

SONGSPIRATION CONTEXT

A great song to get married and dance to. And so it was also used by NASA as a wake-up song on the STS-126 Space Shuttle mission to celebrate the wedding anniversary of astronaut Christopher Ferguson, one of the mission’s crew members.

FEATURED FONTS

Each created in the year of the song release (from top to bottom, left to right)

Harry Obese

Classified and available through
identifont.com

Design: i_dbuero × OA Krimmel
Celebrating: A & O

3

SEPTEMBER

SONG
It’s Now Or Never
ARTIST
Elvis Presley
YEAR
1960

SONGSPIRATION CONTEXT

On this day in 1973, Elvis gave the closing show of his 9th season in Las Vegas. It was an edgy show that blurred the line between the art and the artist. “We kid a lot, and have a lot of fun, but we really love to sing and play music and entertain people ... as long as I can do that I’ll be a happy old sonofabitch!”

FEATURED FONTS

Each created in the year of the song release (from top to bottom, left to right)

Hip Pop NF

Classified and available through
identifont.com

Design: i_dbuero × Carsten Güth
Celebrating: O & A

in the desert

you can't

remember

your name

SEPTEMBER

SONG
A Horse With No Name

ARTIST
America

YEAR
1971

SONGSPIRATION CONTEXT

On this day in 1781, Spanish settlers laid claim to what became Los Angeles, now the second most populous U.S. city and the home to famous Hollywood, whose reknowned name is synonymous with the glamourous motion-picture industry.

FEATURED FONTS

Each created in the year of the song release (from top to bottom, left to right)

JAF Lapture

Classified and available through identifont.com

Design: i_dbuero × OA Krimmel

IS THIS THE
REAL
LIFE
IS THIS JUST
FANTASY

SEPTEMBER

SONG
Bohemian Rhapsody
ARTIST
Queen
YEAR
1975

SONGSPIRATION CONTEXT
On this day in 1946, Farrokh Bulsara born in Zanzibar.
His real life often seemed like a fantasy.
His stage name was Freddie Mercury.

FEATURED FONTS
Each created in the year of the song release (from top to bottom, left to right)

Walbaum

Classified and available through identifont.com

Design: i_dbuero × Sabine Schneider

YOU MAKE MY EARTHQUAKE

6

SEPTEMBER

SONG
Earfquake
ARTIST
Tyler, the Creator
YEAR
2019

SONGSPIRATION CONTEXT

The National Earthquake Information Center now locates about 20,000 earthquakes around the globe each year, or approximately 55 per day.
(The misspelled song title here above isn't a typing error but follows in the grand tradition of such song names as 'Pop Muzik', 'Hot In Herre', 'Grillz' and 'California Gurls').

FEATURED FONTS

Each created in the year of the song release (from top to bottom, left to right)

Ariana Pro

Classified and available through identifont.com

Design: i_dbuero × Evelyn Binder

Hallo

Alles klar?

klar!

SEPTEMBER

SONG
Die Da!?!
ARTIST
Die Fantastischen Vier
YEAR
1992

SONGSPIRATION CONTEXT

'Dieda!?!' is the first single from the second studio album of Die Fantastischen Vier and was released on this day in 1992. It is one of the first commercially successful Deutschrap songs. Fun fact: The cover artwork was created by the SONGSPIRATION makers!

FEATURED FONTS

Each created in the year of the song release (from top to bottom, left to right)

FF Pop

Classified and available through identifont.com

Design: i_dbuero × Suse W

smile will bring a sunshine day

8

SEPTEMBER

SONG
Sunshine Day
ARTIST
Osibisa
YEAR
1975

SONGSPIRATION CONTEXT

It takes eight minutes for sunlight to reach our Earth. The average distance from the Sun to the Earth is about 150 million km. Light travels at 300,000 km per second so dividing one by the other gives you 500 seconds – eight minutes and twenty seconds.

FEATURED FONTS

Each created in the year of the song release (from top to bottom, left to right)

Glowworm

Classified and available through identifont.com

Design: i_dbuero × Sabine Schneider

you'll
never
walk
alone

9

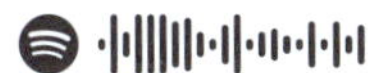

SEPTEMBER

SONG
You'll Never Walk Alone

ARTIST
Gerry & The Peacemakers
(Original: Rodgers/Hammerstein 1945)

YEAR
1963

SONGSPIRATION CONTEXT

The song became famous worldwide in football thanks to The Kop stand at Anfield, the stadium of Liverpool FC. Legend has it that before a match, the stadium's sound system broke down while this song was playing. The fan stand then intoned the song themselves. Since that day, the song has been sung by the crowd before the start of Liverpool matches as the anthem of the club.

FEATURED FONTS

Each created in the year of the song release (from top to bottom, left to right)

Compacta Std

Classified and available through identifont.com

Design: i_dbuero × Sabine Schneider

Futures made of virtual insanity - now

10

SEPTEMBER

SONG
Virtual Insanity
ARTIST
Jamiroquai
YEAR
1996

SONGSPIRATION CONTEXT

Jay Kay is the son of the English cabaret singer Karen Kay and the Portuguese guitarist Luís Saraiva. He only met his biological father in 2001. Kay's identical twin, David, died a few weeks after they were born. At the age of 15, he was homeless and engaged in petty crime to survive; after a false arrest and near-death experience, he returned home, worked as a break dancer and soon pursued a music career. Jay Kay founded Jamiroquai in 1992.

FEATURED FONTS

Each created in the year of the song release (from top to bottom, left to right)

Euphoric

Classified and available through identifont.com

Design: i_dbuero × Carsten Güth

who knows?

ONLY TIME

SEPTEMBER

SONG
Only Time
ARTIST
Enya
YEAR
2000

SONGSPIRATION CONTEXT

A few hours after the 9/11 attacks, the financial broker Steve Golding created a short video using the images that today the whole world knows. It featured the collapsing Twin Towers but above all photos of the victims and the whole human tragedy. The song he put to the video was 'Only time'. Quickly this song became the worldwide mourning hymn, also used by many other TV Networks. Golding died in 2006 at the age of only 50 from an illness triggered at the time by the attacks.

FEATURED FONTS

Each created in the year of the song release (from top to bottom, left to right)

Acetone, Ankora

Classified and available through identifont.com

Design: i_dbuero × Evelyn Binder

You can blow out a candle But you can‘t blow out a

SONG
Biko
ARTIST
Peter Gabriel
YEAR
1980

SONGSPIRATION CONTEXT

'Biko' is an anti-apartheid protest song inspired by the violent death of South African Stephen Bantu Biko. He died on September 12, 1977 in police custody, after being severely beaten during his interrogation. In 2021 a new version was recorded with Peter Gabriel and 25 musicians from 7 countries, *Playing For Change*.

FEATURED FONTS

Each created in the year of the song release (from top to bottom, left to right)

Fenice

Classified and available through identifont.com

Design: i_dbuero × Robert Jähnigen

air
the
in
is
Love

SEPTEMBER

SONG
Love Is In The Air
ARTIST
John Paul Young
YEAR
1977

SONGSPIRATION CONTEXT

"There is always some madness in love.
But there is also always some reason in madness."
(Friedrich Nietzsche)

FEATURED FONTS

Each created in the year of the song release (from top to bottom, left to right)

Harlow Plain

Classified and available through identifont.com

Design: i_dbuero × Björn Börris Peters

What
kind of
FUCKERY
is this?

SONG
Me & Mr. Jones
ARTIST
Amy Winehouse
YEAR
2006

SONGSPIRATION CONTEXT

Amy Winehouse died at just 27 – making her part of the macabre 27 Club, to which many celebrities belong. She died of alcohol poisoning. The night before her death, her family doctor had seen the soul star again. "She said explicitly that she did not want to die". Amy Winehouse had started drinking again "out of boredom". Today we celebrate her birthday (born in 1983).

FEATURED FONTS

Each created in the year of the song release (from top to bottom, left to right)

Valet

Classified and available through identifont.com

Design: i_dbuero × OA Krimmel

It doesn't matter if it's good enough to someone else

15

SEPTEMBER

SONG
The Middle
ARTIST
Jimmy Eat World
YEAR
2001

SONGSPIRATION CONTEXT

The band wrote this song after their old record company kicked them out for being unsuccessful. They called their new album *Bleed American* and found a new record company for it, releasing it in mid-2001. However, after the September 11 attacks, the title of the album was changed to *Jimmy Eat World*.

FEATURED FONTS

Each created in the year of the song release (from top to bottom, left to right)

BD Tatami

Classified and available through identifont.com

Design: i_dbuero × OA Krimmel

What if
there's a
footprint
I left
a life ago

SONG
Footprints
ARTIST
Attack In Black
YEAR
2007

SONGSPIRATION CONTEXT

Today is World Ozone Day. It is also known as the International Day for the Preservation of the Ozone Layer. The ozone layer is a shield of gas that protects the Earth from the harmful rays of the Sun and helps in preserving life on the planet.

FEATURED FONTS

Each created in the year of the song release (from top to bottom, left to right)

Adriane Text

Classified and available through identifont.com

Design: i_dbuero × Sabine Schneider

You've been chosen as an extra in the movie adaptation of the sequel to your life

SONG
Shady Lane

ARTIST
Pavement

YEAR
1997

SONGSPIRATION CONTEXT

Today in 1926, Mexican artist Frida Kahlo was severely injured in a bus accident, and during her recovery she began painting and soon abandoned her plans for a career in medicine.

FEATURED FONTS

Each created in the year of the song release (from top to bottom, left to right)

BD Lo-Fi, BD Kristallo

Classified and available through identifont.com

Design: i_dbuero × Syl Hillier

BECOMES
a better one

SONG
7 Years
ARTIST
Lukas Graham
YEAR
2015

SONGSPIRATION CONTEXT

Today's birthday boy (1988) Lukas Forchhammer, a.k.a. Luke the Duke, is not just from Denmark, but from the state-tolerated autonomous municipality of Christiania. The freetown, just 34 hectares in size, is an alternative housing estate in Copenhagen. The binding rules here are: no hard drugs, no weapons, no violence, no bulletproof clothing, no stolen goods.

FEATURED FONTS

Each created in the year of the song release (from top to bottom, left to right)

Modern Love Caps, Modern Love Grunge, Acumin

Classified and available through identifont.com

Design: i_dbuero × Sarah Meßelken

time's up

19

SEPTEMBER

SONG
He's A Pirate
ARTIST
Klaus Badelt
YEAR
2003

SONGSPIRATION CONTEXT

What be happenin', matey? Today is International Talk Like a Pirate Day. An observer of this holiday would greet friends not with "Hello, everyone!" but with "Ahoy, maties!" or "Ahoy, me hearties!" There's a bit of Jack Sparrow in all of us, isn't there, ye scurvy scum?

FEATURED FONTS

Each created in the year of the song release (from top to bottom, left to right)

Lord Rat

Classified and available through identifont.com

Design: i_dbuero × Evelyn Binder

I can dig it
he can dig it
she
can dig it
we can dig it
they can dig it
oh let's dig it

SONG
Grazing In The Grass
ARTIST
Friends of Distinction
YEAR
1969

SONGSPIRATION CONTEXT

This was the very first big hit to incorporate "dig it" into the lyrics, preceding the famous 'Theme From Shaft' ("Can ya dig it?"), or 'Saturday In The Park' ("Can you dig it? Yes, I can") and a few others. Group member Harry Elston wrote the lyric, which was inspired by his time on Ray Charles' tour when he would look out the window and see cows as they proceeded to the next stop. These cows got it made, he thought.
(songfacts.com)

FEATURED FONTS

Each created in the year of the song release (from top to bottom, left to right)

Didoni

Classified and available through identifont.com

Design: i_dbuero × OA Krimmel

YOU MAY SAY I'M A DREAMER

BUT I'M NOT THE ONLY ONE

SEPTEMBER

SONG
Imagine
ARTIST
John Lennon
YEAR
1971

SONGSPIRATION CONTEXT

IMAGINE PEACE
(Today is World Peace Day)

FEATURED FONTS

Each created in the year of the song release (from top to bottom, left to right)

Jackson MN

Classified and available through
identifont.com

Design: i_dbuero × Sabine Schneider

TONIGHT'S THE NIGHT

LET'S LIVE IT UP

SEPTEMBER

SONG
I Gotta Feeling
ARTIST
Black Eyed Peas
YEAR
2009

SONGSPIRATION CONTEXT

Will.i.am explained that he wrote the song within an hour after standing on the steps of the Lincoln Memorial at the inauguration of President Obama. He said: "Nobody asked me to write 'I Gotta Feeling.' It just came."

FEATURED FONTS

Each created in the year of the song release (from top to bottom, left to right)

Marzo, Debacle

Classified and available through identifont.com

Design: i_dbuero × Evelyn Binder

IGNORANCE IS BLISS I'M A HAPPY IDIOT

SEPTEMBER

SONG
Happy Idiot
ARTIST
TV On The Radio
YEAR
2014

SONGSPIRATION CONTEXT

On the night of September 23-24, 1846, astronomers discovered Neptune, the eighth planet orbiting around the Sun. The discovery was made based on mathematical calculations of its predicted position due to observed perturbations in the orbit of the planet Uranus.

FEATURED FONTS

Each created in the year of the song release (from top to bottom, left to right)

Bend Five

Classified and available through identifont.com

Design: i_dbuero × Carsten Güth

Don't worry
about a thing,

every little thing
is gonna be

alright

Don't worry
about a thing

every little thing
is gonna be

alright

SONG

Three Little Birds

ARTIST

Bob Marley & The Wailers

YEAR

1977

SONGSPIRATION CONTEXT

This uplifting tune from Bob Marley & The Wailers ninth studio album, *Exodus*, is famous for its reassuring refrain, “Don't worry 'bout a thing, 'cause every little thing is gonna be alright” – a message Marley received from the birds that frequented his porch stoop in Kingston, Jamaica. “That really happened,” he told *Sounds* magazine. “That's where I get my inspiration.” (songfacts.com)

FEATURED FONTS

Each created in the year of the song release (from top to bottom, left to right)

Poppl Residenz, ITC Benguiat

Classified and available through identifont.com

Design: i_dbuero × Syl Hillier

Right
now,
hey
It's
your
to-
mor-
row

25

SEPTEMBER

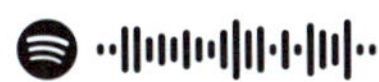

SONG
The World Is Yours
ARTIST
Nas
YEAR
1994

SONGSPIRATION CONTEXT

On this day in 1906, Leonardo Torres y Quevedo demonstrates the *Telekino*, guiding a boat from the shore, in what is considered to be the first use of a remote control.

FEATURED FONTS

Each created in the year of the song release (from top to bottom, left to right)

FF Dirty One

Classified and available through identifont.com

Design: i_dbuero × Carsten Güth

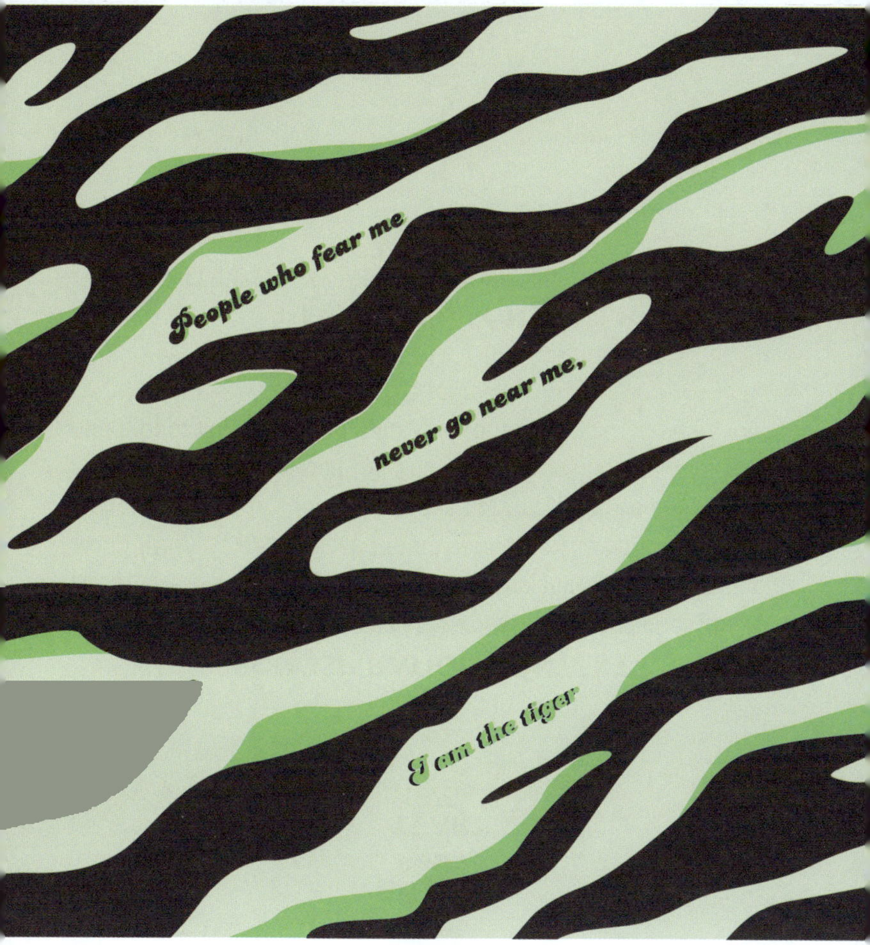

People who fear me

never go near me,

I am the tiger

SONG
Tiger
ARTIST
Abba
YEAR
1976

SONGSPIRATION CONTEXT

Until the release of *ABBA Live at Wembley* on September 26, 2014, *ABBA Live* was for 28 years, the only official live album of the pop group ABBA. It was released four years after the band's temporary split at the end of 1982. The release of the 1986 live album led to speculation worldwide at the time about a possible reunion of the pop group. But in the end, fans had to wait almost 36 years longer for the reunion.

FEATURED FONTS

Each created in the year of the song release (from top to bottom, left to right)

Candice

Classified and available through identifont.com

Design: i_dbuero × OA Krimmel

Sometimes
all i think about
is
you

SONG
Heat Waves
ARTIST
Glass Animals
YEAR
2020

SONGSPIRATION CONTEXT

The music video shows Bayley carting an amp in a wagon through London. He reaches an empty music hall and performs this song with the rest of the band. Bayley called the video "a love letter to live music and the culture and togetherness surrounding it." The band recorded the video for the song during the COVID-19 pandemic. Their neighbors filmed it on their own phones. (songfacts.com)

FEATURED FONTS

Each created in the year of the song release (from top to bottom, left to right)

Geminian

Classified and available through identifont.com

Design: i_dbuero × Syl Hillier

Oh a leopard
can't change
his spots

SONG
Change Of Heart
ARTIST
Dean Martin
YEAR
1955

SONGSPIRATION CONTEXT

"The whole world is drunk and we're just the cocktail of the moment. Someday soon, the world will wake up, down two aspirin with a glass of tomato juice, and wonder what the hell all the fuss was about."
(Dean Martin)

FEATURED FONTS

Each created in the year of the song release (from top to bottom, left to right)
Filmotype Hudson

Classified and available through identifont.com

Design: i_dbuero × OA Krimmel

On days
In times
like this
like these
I feel
an animal
deep inside

SONG
This Corrosion
ARTIST
The Sisters Of Mercy
YEAR
1985

SONGSPIRATION CONTEXT

The band shares its name with an order of Catholic nuns, but Eldritch and Marx took it from Leonard Cohen's 1967 song 'Sisters of Mercy' which they heard in the Robert Altman film *McCabe & Mrs. Miller*, starring Warren Beatty and Julie Christie. Eldritch (*Sounds*, 1987):"I took it from the Leonard Cohen song which is all about prostitutes and I thought the balance between nuns and prostitutes was very appropriate for a rock band, still do."

FEATURED FONTS

Each created in the year of the song release (from top to bottom, left to right)

Corporate A & S

Classified and available through identifont.com

Design: i_dbuero × Evelyn Binder

I'M IN LÖVE WITH ROCK 'N' ROLL
IT SATISFIES MY SOUL
IF THAT'S HOW IT HAS TO BE,
I WON'T GET MAD

SONG
Rock 'n' Roll
ARTIST
Motörhead
YEAR
1987

SONGSPIRATION CONTEXT
Originally, rock and roll – or the corresponding progressive form ‘rocking and rolling’, is a slang expression and euphemism especially for coitus ...

FEATURED FONTS
Each created in the year of the song release (from top to bottom, left to right)

Letraset Arta

Classified and available through identifont.com

Design: i_dbuero × Martin Drozmann

Please don't stop the music music music

1

OCTOBER

SONG
Don‘t Stop the Music
ARTIST
Rihanna
YEAR
2007

SONGSPIRATION CONTEXT

If you bought this calendar (or got it as a gift), then we can certainly all agree that music is one of the best things mankind has ever invented. Today, this is officially celebrated with the UNESCO World Music Day. “mama-say mama-sa mama-ko-sa”, which means: let’s dance…
(thanks to Manu Dibango‘s Soul Makossa)

FEATURED FONTS

Each created in the year of the song release (from top to bottom, left to right)

Black Sabbath

Classified and available through identifont.com

Design: i_dbuero × Carsten Güth

My *Love* is stronger than your HATE will ever be

2

OCTOBER

SONG
Shooting Stars
ARTIST
Rival Sons
YEAR
2017

SONGSPIRATION CONTEXT

Today is the International Day of Non-Violence. It is observed on 2 October to mark the birthday of Mahatma Gandhi who had played an important role in movement of non-violence.

FEATURED FONTS

Each created in the year of the song release (from top to bottom, left to right)

Blackest Text, Gelato Script, Gold under the Mud

Classified and available through identifont.com

Design: i_dbuero × Carsten Güth

3

OCTOBER

SONG
The Whole of the Moon
ARTIST
The Waterboys
YEAR
1985

SONGSPIRATION CONTEXT

The first full moon after the Harvest Moon quite often falls in October and even has its own name. Known as the Hunter's Moon, it's one of the only two full moons (along with the Harvest Moon) that aren't connected to a specific month.

FEATURED FONTS

Each created in the year of the song release (from top to bottom, left to right)

Corporate E BQ

Classified and available through identifont.com

Design: i_dbuero × Carsten Güth

DU

~~MUSST~~*

*~~GAR NIX~~

SONG
Du musst gar nix
ARTIST
Die Sterne
YEAR
2021

SONGSPIRATION CONTEXT

You don't have to change your mind / You don't have to have an opinion at all / You don't have to do *anything* / You don't have to plan / You don't have to piss / You don't have to get up / You don't have to go to bed / You don't have to talk / No way do you have to answer questions / You don't have to ask any questions / You don't have to take your cue from the next best idiot / You can also get lost all by yourself ...

FEATURED FONTS

Each created in the year of the song release (from top to bottom, left to right)

Operetta

Classified and available through identifont.com

Design: i_dbuero × Sabine Schneider

WE LEARNED MORE FROM A THREE MINUTE RECORD THAN WE EVER LEARNED IN SCHOOL

SONG
No Surrender
ARTIST
Bruce Springsteen
YEAR
1986

SONGSPIRATION CONTEXT

UNESCO proclaimed 5 October World Teachers' Day in 1994. It commemorates the ILO/UNESCO Recommendation on the Status of Teachers (1966) and the important role of teachers in quality education.

FEATURED FONTS

Each created in the year of the song release (from top to bottom, left to right)

Citizen

Classified and available through identifont.com

Design: i_dbuero × Carsten Güth

THE FIRST CUT IS THE DEEPEST

6

OCTOBER

SONG
The First Cut is the Deepest

ARTIST
Rod Stewart

YEAR
1976

SONGSPIRATION CONTEXT
On this day in 1889, the Moulin Rouge in Paris opened its doors to the public for the first time.

FEATURED FONTS
Each created in the year of the song release (from top to bottom, left to right)

Frutiger

Classified and available through identifont.com

Design: i_dbuero × Sabine Schneider

I'VE
GOT
Sunshine
ON A
cloudy day

SONG
My Girl
ARTIST
The Temptations
YEAR
1965

SONGSPIRATION CONTEXT

"I've learned over the years that people are human and have mood swings, regardless of how talented they are. Today, I'm looking at life from a realistic point of view instead of the way I would want things to be."

(Band leader Otis Williams)

FEATURED FONTS

Each created in the year of the song release (from top to bottom, left to right)

Davida, P22 Zebra Stencil

Classified and available through identifont.com

Design: i_dbuero × Evelyn Binder

YOU CAN STAND

UNDER MY UMBRELLA

OCTOBER

SONG
Umbrella
ARTIST
Rihanna
YEAR
2007

SONGSPIRATION CONTEXT

The song was originally written with Britney Spears in mind, but her label rejected it. *Entertainment Weekly* ranked the song number one on the 10 Best Singles of 2007.

FEATURED FONTS

Each created in the year of the song release (from top to bottom, left to right)

Word from Radio

Classified and available through identifont.com

Design: i_dbuero × Carsten Güth

So ein Tag, so wunderschön wie heute

SONG

So ein Tag, so wunderschön wie heute

ARTIST

Ernst Neger

YEAR

1952

SONGSPIRATION CONTEXT

World Post Day is an international day that occurs each year on October 9, the anniversary of the Universal Postal Union (UPU), which started in 1874 in Switzerland.

FEATURED FONTS

Each created in the year of the song release (from top to bottom, left to right)

Melior

Classified and available through identifont.com

Design: i_dbuero × Susanne Wagner

ANOTHER ONE BITES THE DUST

OCTOBER

SONG
Another One Bites The Dust
ARTIST
Queen
YEAR
1980

SONGSPIRATION CONTEXT

With its infectious chorus, 'Another One Bites The Dust' was always going to be a hit. This was much to the fury of Christian evangelists, who believed the song involved a satanic back-masked message in its chorus. Hear Freddie Mercury singing backwards, and there's the simple suggestion of: "It's fun to smoke marijuana." Today is World Mental Health Day.
Check this out on YouTube ...

FEATURED FONTS

Each created in the year of the song release (from top to bottom, left to right)

Baskerville

Classified and available through identifont.com

Design: i_dbuero × Sabine Schneider

OCTOBER

SONG
Tie a Yellow Ribbon 'Round The Ole Oak Tree

ARTIST
Tony Orlando & Dawn

YEAR
1972

SONGSPIRATION CONTEXT

Well, the song is only marginally related to today (Arbor Day) – but the old Oak Tree still plays an important supporting role. And this inferred today's song inspiration should of course not be missing from your SONGSPIRATION Calendar: tree-hugging or lovers-hugging, preferably both.

FEATURED FONTS

Each created in the year of the song release (from top to bottom, left to right)

Buster

Classified and available through identifont.com

Design: i_dbuero × OA Krimmel

The love that you need will never be found at home

12

OCTOBER

SONG
Smalltown Boy
ARTIST
Bronski Beat
YEAR
1984

SONGSPIRATION CONTEXT

Time Out ranked “Smalltown Boy” number 12 in their list of The 50 Best Gay Songs to Celebrate Pride All Year Long in 2022.

FEATURED FONTS

Each created in the year of the song release (from top to bottom, left to right)

Octa

Classified and available through identifont.com

Design: i_dbuero × Jana Steffen

GIRLS WILL BE BOYS

&

BOYS WILL BE GIRLS

OCTOBER

SONG
Lola
ARTIST
The Kinks
YEAR
1970

SONGSPIRATION CONTEXT

October 13 is No Bra Day.

FEATURED FONTS

Each created in the year of the song release (from top to bottom, left to right)

Zipper, Machine

Classified and available through
identifont.com

Design: i_dbuero × Carsten Güth

BUT YOU'LL
NEVER FIND
PEACE OF MIND
'TIL YOU LISTEN
TO YOUR
HEART

SONG
Kissing A Fool
ARTIST
George Michael
YEAR
1988

SONGSPIRATION CONTEXT

Winnie-the-Pooh by A.A. Milne, with illustrations by E.H. Shepard, was first published on October 14, 1926.

FEATURED FONTS

Each created in the year of the song release (from top to bottom, left to right)

Refracta

Classified and available through identifont.com

Design: i_dbuero × Carsten Güth

YOU'RE GONNA BE THE ONE THAT SAVES ME

SONG
Wonderwall
ARTIST
Oasis
YEAR
1995

SONGSPIRATION CONTEXT

By the way, you can look in vain for the word "Wonderwall" in the English dictionary, because it does not exist as such.
But there is a clear connection to the Beatles: John Lennon once used the term in an interview instead of the word "wonderful" and his band colleague George Harrison released his first solo album entitled *Wonderwall Music* in 1968, the soundtrack to the film *Wonderwall*. In the film, a man falls in love with the woman next door, played by film icon Jane Birkin, and starts drilling holes in the wall so he can watch her.

FEATURED FONTS

Each created in the year of the song release (from top to bottom, left to right)

Chromosome

Classified and available through identifont.com

Design: i_dbuero × Tim Oliver Schweizer

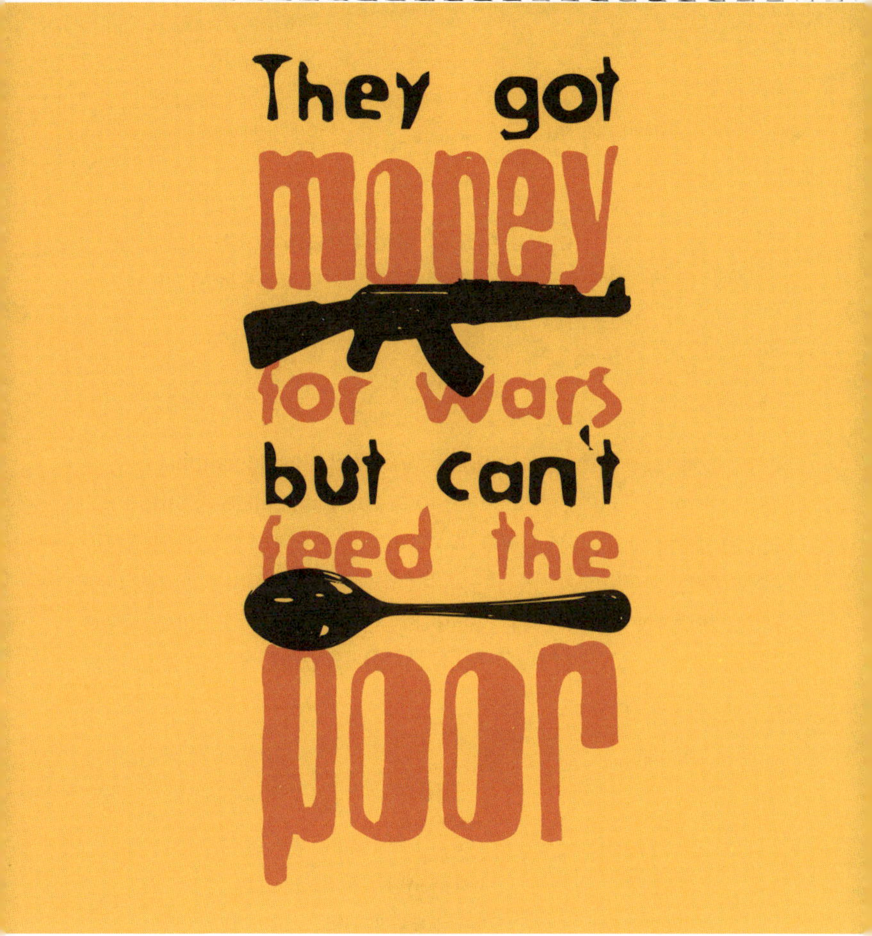

They got money for wars but can't feed the poor

OCTOBER

SONG
Keep Ya Head Up

ARTIST
2Pac

YEAR
1993

SONGSPIRATION CONTEXT

World Food Day (WFD) was established by United Nations FAO's Member Countries at the Organization's 20th General Conference in 1979. It has since been observed every year in more than 150 countries, raising awareness of the issues behind poverty and hunger. Have a look: www.actionagainsthunger.org

FEATURED FONTS

Each created in the year of the song release (from top to bottom, left to right)

Outta Here, Harlem Slang

Classified and available through identifont.com

Design: i_dbuero × Carsten Güth

17

OCTOBER

SONG
There's A Tear In My Beer
ARTIST
Hank Williams, Hank Williams Jr.
YEAR
1950/1988

SONGSPIRATION CONTEXT
On this day in 1810, the first *Oktoberfest* was held in Munich. 140 years later the original version of this country song was written and recorded by Hank Williams, but he never released it. Many years later, in 1988, his son did an electronic duet version with his deceased father and they both "shared" a Grammy for it.

FEATURED FONTS
Each created in the year of the song release (from top to bottom, left to right)

Variex OT

Classified and available through identifont.com

Design: i_dbuero × Evelyn Binder

forget the
{cage}
'cause
we
know
how to
make
the
key

SONG
The Other Side

ARTIST
Zac Efron, Hugh Jackman

YEAR
2017

SONGSPIRATION CONTEXT

According to *The Times*, Zac Efron said:
"Amazingly, when I signed up for Tinder, nobody swiped me!
They thought [my profile] was fake."
Happy birthday Zac.

FEATURED FONTS

Each created in the year of the song release (from top to bottom, left to right)

Halyard

Classified and available through
identifont.com

Design: i_dbuero × Sabine Schneider

If you
wanna have a
good
time
just give me
a call

SONG
Don‘t Stop Me Now
ARTIST
Queen
YEAR
1978

SONGSPIRATION CONTEXT

Today is International Gin and Tonic Day. The cocktail idea began during the reign of the British East India Company in India during the 1700s. Malaria had been roaming around in India and became a problem. George Cleghorn, a Scottish doctor, discovered that quinine, a flavor component of tonic water, could be used to treat malaria. However, not many liked the taste. So, British officers in India in the early 1800s began adding water, sugar, lime, and gin to the tonic water, and thus the gin and tonic was born.

FEATURED FONTS

Each created in the year of the song release (from top to bottom, left to right)

Harlow, VAG Rounded

Classified and available through identifont.com

Design: i_dbuero × Sabine Schneider

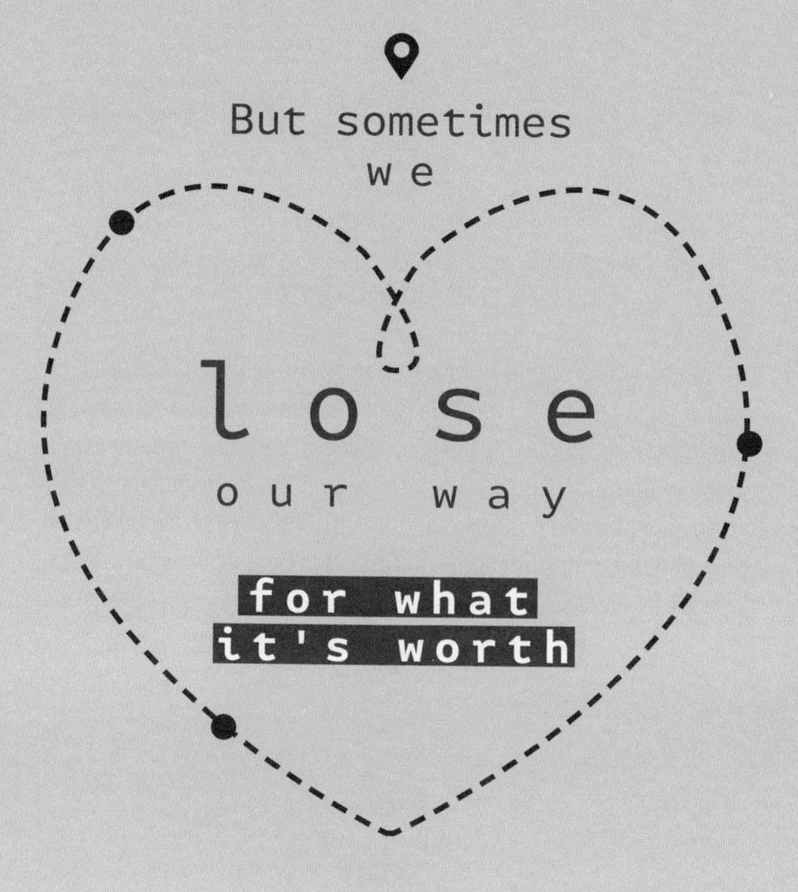
But sometimes
we
lose
our way
for what
it's worth

SONG
For What It's Worth
ARTIST
Liam Gallagher
YEAR
2017

SONGSPIRATION CONTEXT

Liam Gallagher is known as a bad boy because of his many escapades. The ex-Oasis singer has repeatedly attracted attention through drug and alcohol excesses, quarrels with his brother and band colleague Noel Gallagher, insults – and fights. During a mass brawl in Munich in December 2002, Liam Gallagher even lost two incisors. Gallagher and four other band members had to spend a night at a police station. Oasis' originally planned tour of Germany had to be cancelled.

FEATURED FONTS

Each created in the year of the song release (from top to bottom, left to right)

Attribute Mono

Classified and available through identifont.com

Design: i_dbuero × Sabine Schneider

I need

perfection

some

twisted

selection

SONG
Mystify
ARTIST
INXS
YEAR
1987

SONGSPIRATION CONTEXT

Every year the exquisite orchards spill forth a cavalcade of crimson, gold, and green, and it's not just the leaves of autumn. On the heels of this rolling bounty comes the rich smell of apple pies, spicy ciders (both alcoholic and not), and all the tastes and smells of this seasonal treat. This is the time to celebrate everything that has to do with National Apple Day!

FEATURED FONTS

Each created in the year of the song release (from top to bottom, left to right)

Goudy Old Style

Classified and available through identifont.com

Design: i_dbuero × Carsten Güth

La, la, la, la, la, la, la.

I JUST CAN'T GET YOU OUT OF MY HEAD...

OCTOBER

SONG
Can‘t Get You Out Of My Head

ARTIST
Kylie Minogue

YEAR
2001

SONGSPIRATION CONTEXT

On this day in 2012, Australian singer Kylie Minogue attended the Q Awards at Grosvenor House in London. It’s not particularly remarkable, but I just can’t get it out of my head.

FEATURED FONTS

Each created in the year of the song release (from top to bottom, left to right)

Archer

Classified and available through identifont.com

Design: i_dbuero × Sabine Schneider

Freedom's just another word for nothing left to lose.

SONG
Me And Bobby McGee
ARTIST
Janis Joplin
YEAR
1971

SONGSPIRATION CONTEXT

Tomorrow in 1933, the notorious criminal John Dillinger and his gang rob a Greencastle, Indiana bank of $74,802. It was their largest bank robbery. It is claimed that when Dillinger saw a farmer at a teller with cash, he asked the farmer if it was his or the bank's money. The farmer replied it was his life savings. Dillinger, a farm boy, replied, "Keep it. We only want the bank's money."

FEATURED FONTS

Each created in the year of the song release (from top to bottom, left to right)

Lapture

Classified and available through identifont.com

Design: i_dbuero × Pia Bardesono

I KEEP DANCING ON MY

OCTOBER

SONG
Dancing On My Own
ARTIST
Robyn
YEAR
2010

SONGSPIRATION CONTEXT

On this day in 1901: The first successful barrel ride over Niagara Falls occurred when Anna Edson Taylor, a school teacher, rode safely over the Falls in a barrel. The ride through the rapids took 18 minutes.

FEATURED FONTS

Each created in the year of the song release (from top to bottom, left to right)

Fun City

Classified and available through identifont.com

Design: i_dbuero × Carsten Güth

I'm the

BAD GUY

25

OCTOBER

SONG
Bad Guy
ARTIST
Billie Eilish
YEAR
2019

SONGSPIRATION CONTEXT

"If I make music and people hate it, you know, whatever. I'll die someday, and one day, they will too."
(Billie Eilish)

FEATURED FONTS

Each created in the year of the song release (from top to bottom, left to right)

Ansage Variable

Classified and available through identifont.com

Design: i_dbuero × Syl Hillier

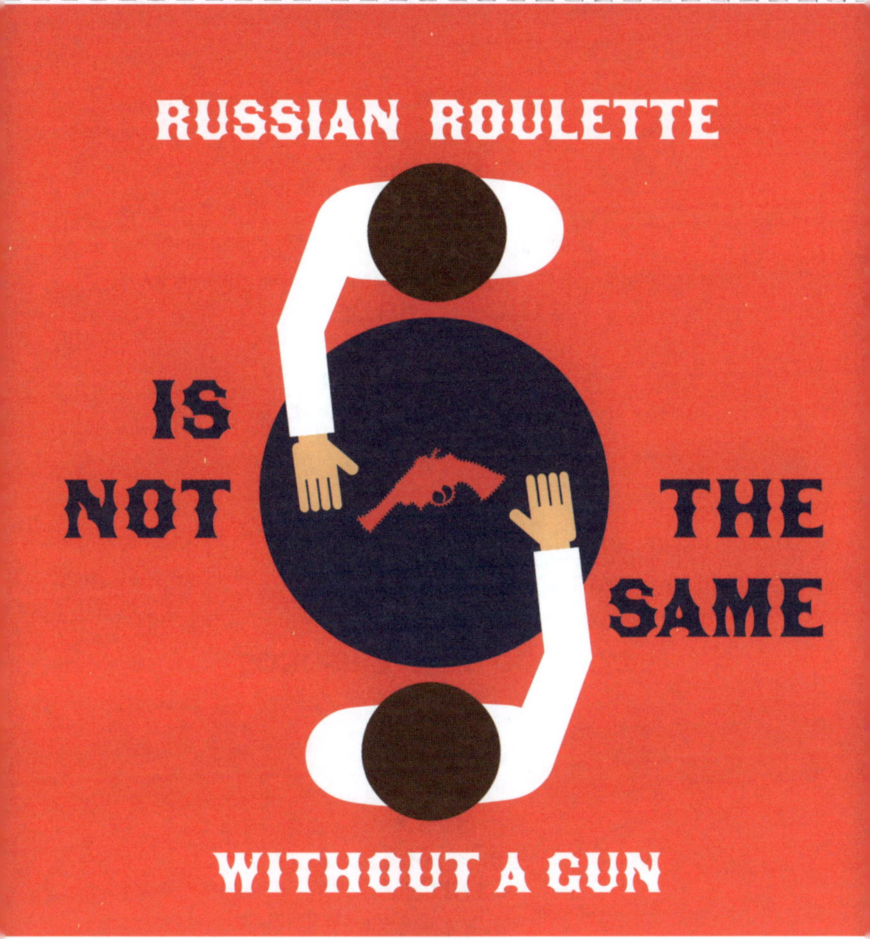

RUSSIAN ROULETTE

IS NOT THE SAME

WITHOUT A GUN

OCTOBER

SONG
Poker Face
ARTIST
Lady Gaga
YEAR
2013

SONGSPIRATION CONTEXT

The 'Mum-mum-mum-ma' hook sounds familiar to you? No wonder – it's from Boney M's 1977 hit 'Ma Baker'. But of course Poker Face Lady Gaga has a few other trump cards up her sleeve.

FEATURED FONTS

Each created in the year of the song release (from top to bottom, left to right)

Becker Gothics Concave

Classified and available through identifont.com

Design: i_dbuero × OA Krimmel

My life is a movie

SONG
Old Town Road
ARTIST
Lil Nas X
YEAR
2018

SONGSPIRATION CONTEXT

"Just because you like one song from an artist, that doesn't make you a fan." – Lil Nas X

FEATURED FONTS

Each created in the year of the song release (from top to bottom, left to right)

Ohno Blazeface, Bimbo

Classified and available through identifont.com

Design: i_dbuero × Evelyn Binder

you're
the one
yes
you are

SONG
Cuba
ARTIST
The Gibson Brothers
YEAR
1979

SONGSPIRATION CONTEXT

On this day in 1492, Christopher Columbus discovered Cuba – and christened it 'Juana', in honor of the Spanish Queen Isabella's son, Prince Don Juan.

FEATURED FONTS

Each created in the year of the song release (from top to bottom, left to right)

Rhode Normal, Corpid, Chauncy Fatty

Classified and available through identifont.com

Design: i_dbuero × Evelyn Binder

STEREO

SIDE 1

90

LOSE YOUR DREAM,
AND YOU WILL LOSE YOUR MIND

OCTOBER

SONG
Ruby Tuesday
ARTIST
The Rolling Stones
YEAR
1967

SONGSPIRATION CONTEXT

The Roaring Twenties came to an abrupt end on 29 October, "Black Tuesday", part of the Wall Street Crash in 1929, which ushered in a worldwide economic crisis. The Stones' song is fortunately the opposite, namely a roaring success: A beautiful love song Keith Richards wrote for a groupie, his first steady girlfriend, Linda Keith. SONGSPIRATION says: No more Black Tuesdays, but rather more Ruby Tuesdays.

FEATURED FONTS

Each created in the year of the song release (from top to bottom, left to right)

Mauritius

Classified and available through identifont.com

Design: i_dbuero × OA Krimmel

It's Tricky

TRICKY

30

OCTOBER

SONG
It's Tricky
ARTIST
Run-D.M.C.
YEAR
1986

SONGSPIRATION CONTEXT

Band co-founder Jam Master Jay died in an assassination attempt on 30 October 2002. The case remained unsolved for almost two decades until finally, in 2020, two men were charged with his murder. The defendants allegedly committed the crime because of a cocaine deal in which the victim was involved and a dispute over distribution had arisen.

FEATURED FONTS

Each created in the year of the song release (from top to bottom, left to right)

Bronx, Insignia

Classified and available through identifont.com

Design: i_dbuero × OA Krimmel

You bleed just to know you're alive

OCTOBER

SONG
Iris
ARTIST
The Goo Goo Dolls
YEAR
1998

SONGSPIRATION CONTEXT

Trick or treat!

This night is HALLOWEEN!

(incidentally short for All Hallow's Eve (All Saints' Eve))

FEATURED FONTS

Each created in the year of the song release (from top to bottom, left to right)

Cocon

Classified and available through identifont.com

Design: i_dbuero × Pia Bardesono

it's better to burn out than to

NOVEMBER

SONG
Hey Hey, My, My (Into the Black)
ARTIST
Neil Young
YEAR
1979

SONGSPIRATION CONTEXT

Today is Day of the Dead. Former Nirvana frontman Kurt Cobain took his own life in 1994 and, in the final letter he left to his fans, friends and family, reprinted this phrase "It's better to burn out than to fade away". Neil Young commented on this: "Being mentioned in Kurt Cobain's suicide note fucked with me".

FEATURED FONTS

Each created in the year of the song release (from top to bottom, left to right)

Milka, Milka Aged

Classified and available through identifont.com

Design: i_dbuero × OA Krimmel

if I
ruled
the
world,
imagine
that

2

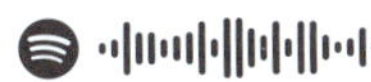

NOVEMBER

SONG
If I Ruled The World

ARTIST
Nas

YEAR
1996

SONGSPIRATION CONTEXT

Marie-Antoinette was born on 2 November 1755 at the Hofburg Palace in Vienna, Austria. “Let them eat cake” is the most famous quote attributed to Marie-Antoinette, the queen of France during the French Revolution. As the story goes, it was the queen’s response upon being told that her starving peasant subjects had no bread.

FEATURED FONTS

Each created in the year of the song release (from top to bottom, left to right)

Klepto ITC

Classified and available through identifont.com

Design: i_dbuero × Carsten Güth

Holding out for a HERO

3

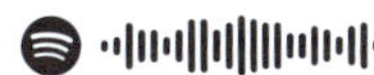

NOVEMBER

SONG
Holding Out For A Hero

ARTIST
Bonnie Tyler

YEAR
1984

SONGSPIRATION CONTEXT

Today is International Men's Day! Bonnie Tyler is looking for the right man in her song. He should also be a hero at the same time. "A streetwise Hercules to fight the rising odds ... larger than life". Apparently she has found him, because since 1973 she has been married to the British judoka Robert Sullivan.

FEATURED FONTS

Each created in the year of the song release (from top to bottom, left to right)

Zwart, Horndon Becker

Classified and available through identifont.com

Design: i_dbuero × Evelyn Binder

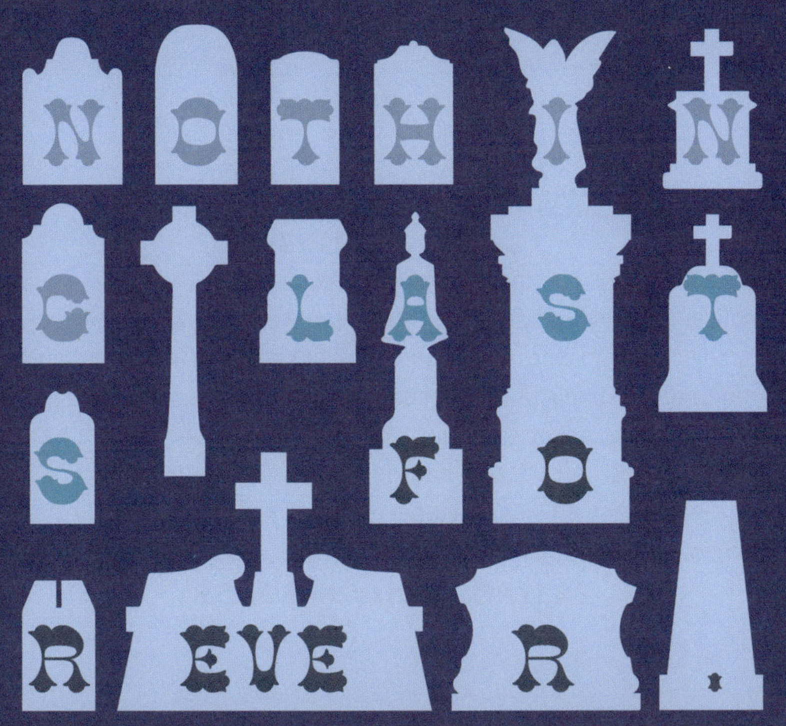

NOTHIN
CLAST
S FO
R EVER R.

SONG
November Rain
ARTIST
Guns N' Roses
YEAR
1991

SONGSPIRATION CONTEXT

Nothing lasts forever – although this love ballad by Axl Rose comes close. Not only because it is eternally long, namely almost 10 minutes. Also because the accompanying video is one of the 20 most expensive music videos ever made and, with more than 1.2 billion views, also one of the most watched videos on YouTube. But above all, because this song about heartbreak has become a timeless evergreen; even today it is played hundreds of thousands of times a day worldwide.

FEATURED FONTS

Each created in the year of the song release (from top to bottom, left to right)

Cottonwood

Classified and available through identifont.com

Design: i_dbuero × OA Krimmel

I'D
RATHER BE
a hammer than a
NAIL

SONG
El Condor Pasa

ARTIST
Simon and Garfunkel

YEAR
1970

SONGSPIRATION CONTEXT

Simon & Garfunkel (his birthday is today!) began recording together as a duo in high school named Tom & Jerry, after the famous cartoon cat and mouse. In 1956, they released their first single 'Hey Schoolgirl', which made it into the Top 50. Already as 16-year-olds, they had hit the nail on the head.

FEATURED FONTS

Each created in the year of the song release (from top to bottom, left to right)

Avant Garde

Classified and available through identifont.com

Design: i_dbuero × OA Krimmel

DAS SYSTEM
IST DEFEKT ________ DIE GESELLSCHAFT
VERSAGT

ABER ALLES WIRD GUT

6

NOVEMBER

SONG
Der letzte Song (Alles wird gut)
ARTIST
Felix Kummer feat. Fred Rabe
YEAR
2021

SONGSPIRATION CONTEXT
Everything is going to be alright. On this day in 1860, Americans elected as their president Abraham Lincoln, whose victory led to the secession of Southern states and the long and bloody Civil War that lasted until 1865 and ended slavery in the U.S.

FEATURED FONTS
Each created in the year of the song release (from top to bottom, left to right)

Wagon

Classified and available through identifont.com

Design: i_dbuero × Sabine Schneider

YOU WANT IT DARKER

WE KILL THE FLAME

NOVEMBER

SONG
You Want It Darker
ARTIST
Leonard Cohen
YEAR
2016

SONGSPIRATION CONTEXT

On November 7, 2016, Leonard Cohen passed away, aged 82. His album *You want it darker* was released only 3 weeks before and it became a great success.

FEATURED FONTS

Each created in the year of the song release (from top to bottom, left to right)

Arca Majora

Classified and available through identifont.com

Design: i_dbuero × Evelyn Binder

WHAT´S
THE
MATTER
WITH THE
W$RLD
T0DAY?

SONG
Call My Name
ARTIST
Prince
YEAR
2004

SONGSPIRATION CONTEXT

Despite trailing in most polls, Republican Donald Trump was elected the 45th president of the United States, though his Democratic opponent, Hillary Clinton, won the popular vote by more than 2.8 million.

FEATURED FONTS

Each created in the year of the song release (from top to bottom, left to right)

State Machine

Classified and available through identifont.com

Design: i_dbuero × Ralph Rieker

MMMBOP DUBA DOPBA DU BOP, BA DUBA DOPBA DU BOP, BA DUBA DOPBA DU, OH YEAH

SONG
MMMBop
ARTIST
Hanson
YEAR
1997

SONGSPIRATION CONTEXT

Today is World Freedom Day. Commemorate the fall of the Berlin Wall and the Iron Curtain and call for liberty everywhere through protest and political activism.

FEATURED FONTS

Each created in the year of the song release (from top to bottom, left to right)

Autotrace , Abaton ITC, Arbuckle Remix NF

Classified and available through identifont.com

Design: i_dbuero × Sabine Schneider

The less I know the better

10 NOVEMBER

SONG
The Less I Know The Better
ARTIST
Tame Impala
YEAR
2015

SONGSPIRATION CONTEXT

November 10 is Forget-Me-Not Day
as well as Sesame Street Day.

FEATURED FONTS

Each created in the year of the song release (from top to bottom, left to right)

LeOsler

Classified and available through
identifont.com

Design: i_dbuero × Carsten Güth

THIS IS MY IDEA OF FUN PLAYIN' VIDEO GAMES

11

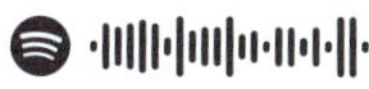

NOVEMBER

SONG
Video Games
ARTIST
Lana Del Rey
YEAR
2012

SONGSPIRATION CONTEXT

On the 11th day in the 11th month at 11 a.m., the foolish time, the carnival, begins in many places. The "11" is considered the most foolish of the numbers. This mainly has to do with its position exactly between two overpowering symbols in biblical number mysticism. The "10", as the number of the commandments and the world order. And then "12": the number of Jesus' apostles and the symbol for new beginnings – like the year that ends after twelve months and starts all over again.

FEATURED FONTS

Each created in the year of the song release (from top to bottom, left to right)

Lichtspiele

Classified and available through identifont.com

Design: i_dbuero × Carsten Güth

Dm
Am
x o o
x o o
1 1fr 1
2 2fr 2 3
3 3fr
4fr
Gm
Fm
o o
1fr 1 1 1 1
2fr
2 3 4 3fr 3 4
4fr

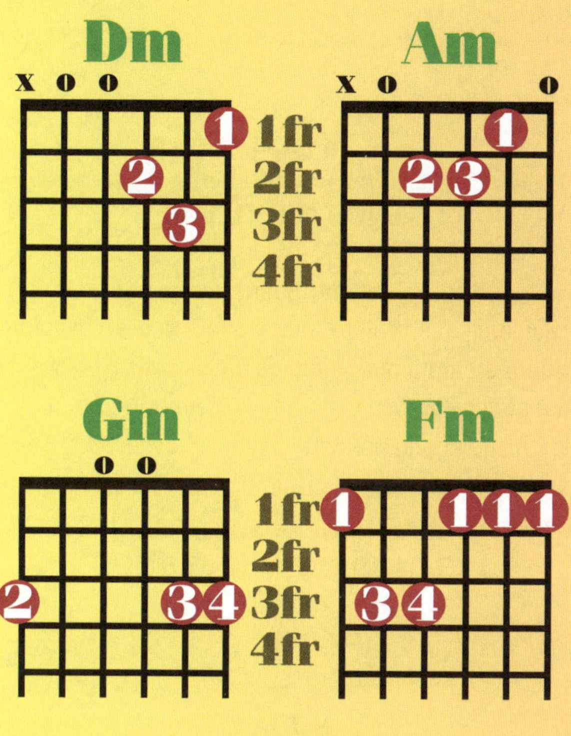

guitar

SONG
Egyptian Reggae

ARTIST
Jonathan Richman & the Modern Lovers

YEAR
1977

SONGSPIRATION CONTEXT

What would SONGSPIRATION be without an instrumental? After all, music can be quite inspiring even without words. Like this 'Egyptian Reggae', for example. Inspired by the environment of Velvet Underground Jonathan Richman had developed a very distinctive style. "His songs are so direct and intimate that he could be confiding in a close friend – and, while you're listening, you feel as if you're that friend yourself". (bbc.com)

FEATURED FONTS

Each created in the year of the song release (from top to bottom, left to right)

Fenice

Classified and available through identifont.com

Design: i_dbuero × OA Krimmel
Celebrating: George

13

NOVEMBER

SONG
Guten Tag
ARTIST
Wir sind Helden
YEAR
2002

SONGSPIRATION CONTEXT

Rarely has consumer criticism sounded so good. Judith Holofernes got it right with her band. »*Guten Tag, guten Tag,* i want my life back« this wish came true. She even added other lives; as a mother, as an author and as a solo artist. She won't get back her birthday (*1976) though, that was yesterday.

FEATURED FONTS

Each created in the year of the song release (from top to bottom, left to right)

FF ZwoPro, Cocktail Shaker

Classified and available through identifont.com

Design: i_dbuero × OA Krimmel
Celebrating: Judith

I' M GIVING YOU A

NIGHT CALL

TO TELL YOU HOW I FEEL

SONG
Nightcall

ARTIST
London Grammar

YEAR
2013

SONGSPIRATION CONTEXT

King Charles III's birthday is today. One of his unpleasant memories is certainly "Camillagate". In an intercepted telephone conversation, the then Prince Charles, still married to Princess Diana, said to his beloved Camilla "I love you". He wished to be closer to her: "I want to feel you everywhere, above you, inside you, under you, inside and outside (...) Oh God, I'll just live inside your trousers or something. It would be much easier." Royal humour, indeed.

FEATURED FONTS

Each created in the year of the song release (from top to bottom, left to right)

Plaak, Faux Orient, Faux Occident

Classified and available through identifont.com

Design: i_dbuero × Carsten Güth

EVERYONE'S
A WINNER
we're making
our
fame

SONG
Paper Planes
ARTIST
M.I.A.
YEAR
2013

SONGSPIRATION CONTEXT

Congrats! You are definitely a winner. You won the sperm race! Scientifically the chances that led to you being born were near zero. For you to have been born, all your great-great-grandfathers and grandmothers must have met at the right place at the right time, multiply that probability by the world population in each era for each of them to have even met in the first place and multiply that amount by the millions of sperms you had to race to get to the egg in order to have been born ... LUCKY YOU!

FEATURED FONTS

Each created in the year of the song release (from top to bottom, left to right)

Vista Slab

Classified and available through identifont.com

Design: i_dbuero × Sabine Schneider

Is jo eh ois, eh

hoid

SONG
Eh Ok
ARTIST
Granada
YEAR
2013

SONGSPIRATION CONTEXT

Why would an Austrian band call itself Granada of all things? This is neither about Latinos nor about the Spanish city of Granada. A lot of time was spent thinking about the right name and looking up suggestions in the dictionary. But finally the band decided on a car, the Ford Granada from the 70s. Cool car, melodic name. Fits well.

FEATURED FONTS

Each created in the year of the song release (from top to bottom, left to right)

Modern Love Grunge, Devinyl Line

Classified and available through identifont.com

Design: i_dbuero × OA Krimmel

Just because you feel it
doesn't mean it's there.

SONG
There, There
ARTIST
Radiohead
YEAR
2003

SONGSPIRATION CONTEXT

It was ceremoniously unveiled in November 1512: the world-famous painting *The Creation of Adam* is the central work of Michelangelo's (Michelangelo Buonarroti, 1475-1564) ceiling fresco, also known as the Genesis fresco. It is one of the most famous depictions in the Sistine Chapel in the Vatican in Rome, commissioned by Pope Julius II.

FEATURED FONTS

Each created in the year of the song release (from top to bottom, left to right)

Avenir

Classified and available through identifont.com

Design: i_dbuero × Sabine Schneider

IF I ONLY COULD I'D MAKE A DEAL WITH GOD AND I'D GET HIM TO

OUR PLACES

SONG
Running Up That Hill (A Deal with God)
ARTIST
Kate Bush
YEAR
1985

SONGSPIRATION CONTEXT

Stranger things happen. For example, “Stranger Things Day” was 12 days ago today. The day when in the series “Will Byers” disappears without a trace. Also a strange thing: The opposite of this happened to Kate Bush’s song thanks to the series: almost 40 years after its release, it resurfaced from obscurity and went to #1 in the UK charts!

FEATURED FONTS

Each created in the year of the song release (from top to bottom, left to right)

Corporate

Classified and available through identifont.com

Design: i_dbuero × Sabine Schneider

oh baby, baby, it`s a

wild world

SONG
Wild World
ARTIST
Cat Stevens
YEAR
1970

SONGSPIRATION CONTEXT

As if 1971 wasn't incredible enough with influential works such as *Sticky Fingers* by the Rolling Stones, *Tapestry* by Carole King, *What's Going On* by Marvin Gaye, *Led Zeppelin IV* or *Imagine* by John Lennon, another wild album is released in November of this unforgettable year that has long since joined the ranks of the absolute classics – *Teaser And The Firecat* by Yusuf/Cat Stevens. It was already his third album in just 18 months.

FEATURED FONTS

Each created in the year of the song release (from top to bottom, left to right)

Avant Garde

Classified and available through identifont.com

Design: i_dbuero × Pia Bardesono

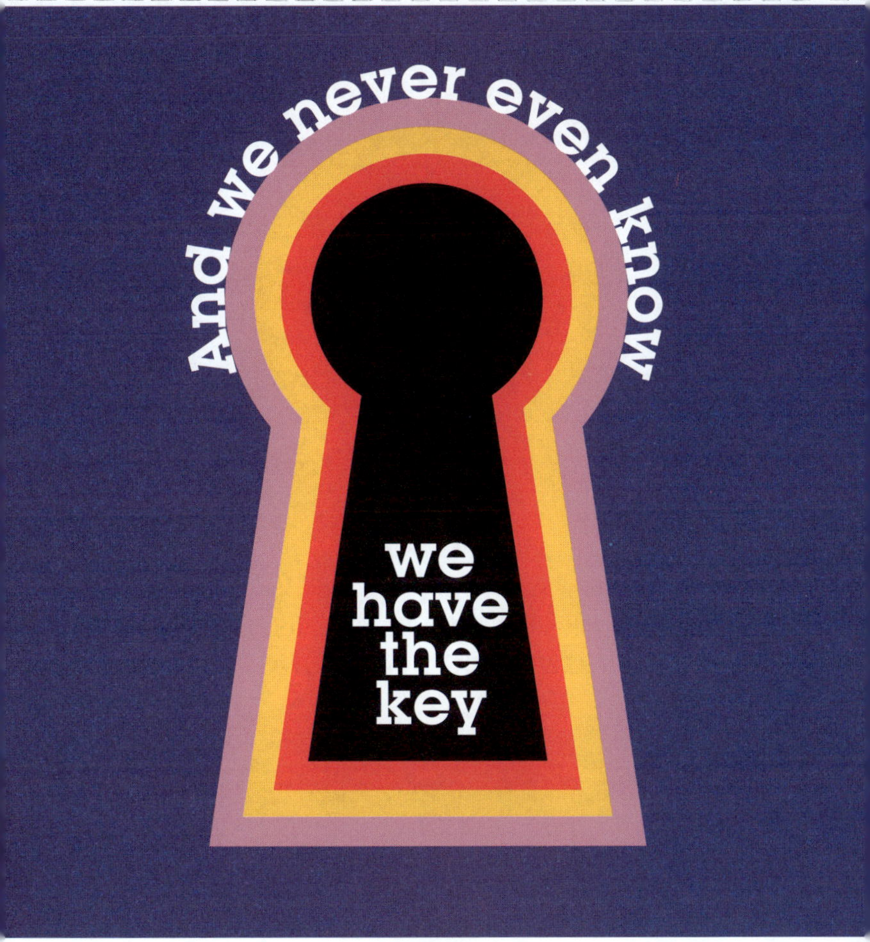

And we never even know

we have the key

NOVEMBER

SONG
Already Gone
ARTIST
Eagles
YEAR
1974

SONGSPIRATION CONTEXT

Today is the birthday of The Eagles guitarist Joseph Fidler "Joe" Walsh. In 2011, *Rolling Stone* listed Walsh as the 54th best guitarist of all time.

FEATURED FONTS

Each created in the year of the song release (from top to bottom, left to right)

ITC Lubalin Graph

Classified and available through identifont.com

Design: i_dbuero × Carsten Güth

FUNNY
HOW A
MELODY
SOUNDS
LIKE A
MEMORY

SONG
Springsteen
ARTIST
Eric Church
YEAR
2011

SONGSPIRATION CONTEXT

Today is World Hello Day. Thirty-one winners of the Nobel Peace Prize have stated that World Hello Day carries substantial value as an instrument for preserving peace. So, go out, create melodies or memories – or at least say hello to someone ...

FEATURED FONTS

Each created in the year of the song release (from top to bottom, left to right)

Ambicase Fatface OT, Abel

Classified and available through identifont.com

Design: i_dbuero × Sabine Schneider

you
and I
have got an
expiration
date

22

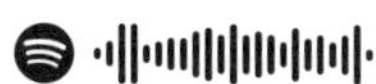

NOVEMBER

SONG
Expiration Date
ARTIST
Michelle
YEAR
2022

SONGSPIRATION CONTEXT

On Friday, November 22, 1963, President John F. Kennedy was shot as he rode in a motorcade through the streets of Dallas, Texas; he died shortly thereafter. The 35th president was 46 years old and had served less than three years in office. During that short time, Kennedy and his wife, Jacqueline Bouvier Kennedy, became immensely popular both at home and abroad.

FEATURED FONTS

Each created in the year of the song release (from top to bottom, left to right)

Dolcissimo Dots

Classified and available through identifont.com

Design: i_dbuero × OA Krimmel

WHAT'S
IN YOUR HEAD,
IN YOUR HEAD
ZOMBIE
ZOMBIE
ZOMBIE-IE-IE

SONG
Zombie
ARTIST
The Cranberries
YEAR
1994

SONGSPIRATION CONTEXT

'Zombie' is considered a protest song against the Northern Ireland conflict. The lyrics of the song were written by The Cranberries in memory of two children killed during an IRA bombing in Warrington in March 1993. Today is Eat A Cranberry Day.

FEATURED FONTS

Each created in the year of the song release (from top to bottom, left to right)

Pleasantly Plump Font

Classified and available through identifont.com

Design: i_dbuero × Sabine Schneider

All I need 's a little sign to get behind the sun

SONG
All I Need
ARTIST
Air
YEAR
1998

SONGSPIRATION CONTEXT

This number was selected as one of the songs to "download and listen to before you die" in the 2010 book *1001 Songs You Must Hear Before You Die.*

FEATURED FONTS

Each created in the year of the song release (from top to bottom, left to right)

Postino

Classified and available through identifont.com

Design: i_dbuero × Carsten Güth

It's a beautiful DAY

Don't let it get away

NOVEMBER

SONG
Beautiful Day
ARTIST
U2
YEAR
2000

SONGSPIRATION CONTEXT

Today is Thanksgiving Day.
"We must find time to stop and thank the people who make a difference in our lives". (John F. Kennedy)
How about today?

FEATURED FONTS

Each created in the year of the song release (from top to bottom, left to right)

Knockout

Classified and available through identifont.com

Design: i_dbuero × Carsten Güth

say what you wanna say

26

NOVEMBER

SONG
Brave
ARTIST
Sara Bareilles
YEAR
2013

SONGSPIRATION CONTEXT

"Here's looking at you kid," he said. Set in occupied Morocco during World War II, directed by Michael Curtiz, and starring Humphrey Bogart, Ingrid Bergman, and Paul Henreid, *Casablanca* premiered this day in 1942 and became one of Hollywood's most-revered films with lots of immortal quotes.

FEATURED FONTS

Each created in the year of the song release (from top to bottom, left to right)

Proxima Nova

Classified and available through identifont.com

Design: i_dbuero × Sabine Schneider

It's the fire inside you

let it burn

27

NOVEMBER

SONG
Fire
ARTIST
The Roots ft. John Legend
YEAR
2010

SONGSPIRATION CONTEXT

"Fire is a song that you could listen to ten times in a row, and still find a new nugget of genius in the lyrics each time. The lyrics are all about keeping your eyes on the prize and meeting every challenge you face." (Natalie Seale) Today is Black Friday.

FEATURED FONTS

Each created in the year of the song release (from top to bottom, left to right)

Condiment, Bunday Slab

Classified and available through identifont.com

Design: i_dbuero × Syl Hillier

LET THE SUNSHINE IN

NOVEMBER

SONG
Aquarius/Let The Sunshine In

ARTIST
The 5th Dimension

YEAR
2010

SONGSPIRATION CONTEXT

"The lyrics of this song medley were based on the astrological belief that the world would soon be entering the "Age of Aquarius", an age of love, light, and humanity. This change was presumed to occur at the end of the 20th century; however, astrologers differ widely as to precisely when." We are waiting impatiently.

FEATURED FONTS

Each created in the year of the song release (from top to bottom, left to right)

Didoni

Classified and available through identifont.com

Design: i_dbuero × Sabine Schneider

THE
future's
so bright,
I GOTTA WEAR
shades

NOVEMBER

SONG
The Future's So Bright, I Gotta Wear Shades
ARTIST
Tibuk 3
YEAR
1986

SONGSPIRATION CONTEXT

In the run-up to the 25th UN Climate Change Conference (COP 25) taking place in Madrid in early December, Fridays For Future demonstrated in 157 countries in 2,400 cities worldwide on 29 November 2019. In Germany alone, demonstrations took place in 500 cities. May our future be bright!

FEATURED FONTS

Each created in the year of the song release (from top to bottom, left to right)

Insignia

Classified and available through identifont.com

Design: i_dbuero × Sabine Schneider

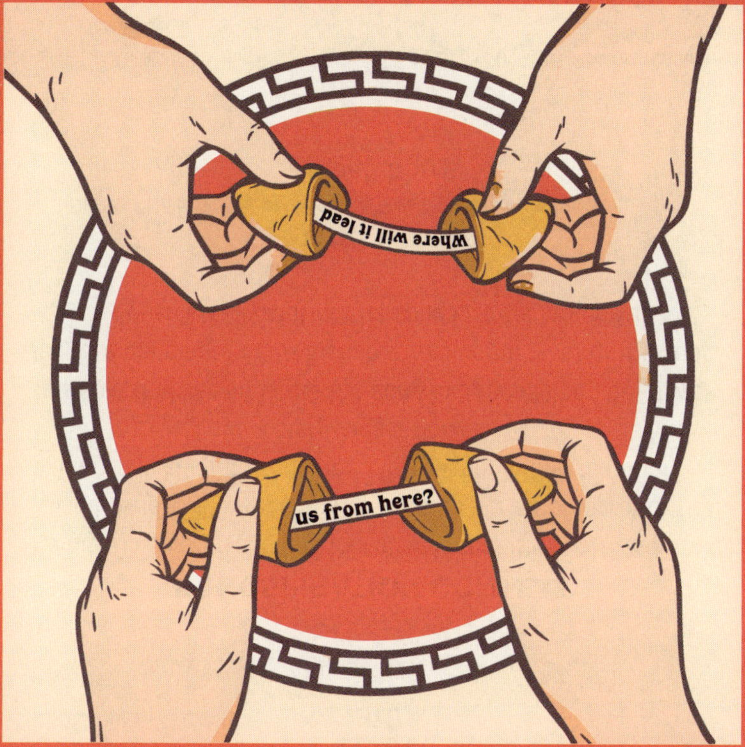

Where will it lead

us from here?

NOVEMBER

SONG
Angie
ARTIST
The Rolling Stones
YEAR
1973

SONGSPIRATION CONTEXT

The big rumour surrounding this song is that it was written about David Bowie's wife Angela, who wrote in her autobiography that she once caught Bowie and Mick Jagger in bed together – a story Jagger denies.
It is said that Jagger wrote the song to appease her, but it was Jagger's bandmate Keith Richards who wrote most of the song. It doesn't really matter, the song is great either way.

FEATURED FONTS

Each created in the year of the song release (from top to bottom, left to right)

Huckleberry

Classified and available through identifont.com

Design: i_dbuero × OA Krimmel
Celebrating: Anja

1

DECEMBER

SONG

It's A Long Way To The Top

ARTIST

AC/DC

YEAR

1975

SONGSPIRATION CONTEXT

"Live. Love. Smile. Hug. Laugh. Dream. Do. Create. Have fun. Be intense. Be audacious. Be unreasonable. Act impeccably. Breathe. Be you. Be different."

(Brian Johnson, singer)

FEATURED FONTS

Each created in the year of the song release (from top to bottom, left to right)

Buxom

Classified and available through identifont.com

Design: i_dbuero × OA Krimmel

ALL YOU TOUCH
AND ALL YOU SEE
IS ALL YOUR LIFE
WILL EVER BE

SONG
Breathe
ARTIST
Pink Floyd
YEAR
1971

SONGSPIRATION CONTEXT

In 1965, Syd Barrett (guitar, vocals), Bob Klose, Rick Wright (keyboards), Nick Mason (drums) and Roger Waters (bass) formed a band called Sigma 6. Klose soon quit, but the other four stayed together for a while. They try out all kinds of band names, The Screaming Abdabs, T-Set, The Meggadeaths, and The Architectural Abdabs, until one day Barrett arrives with the suggestion The Pink Floyd Sound, which is based on the first names of the two jazz musicians Pink Anderson and Floyd Council.

FEATURED FONTS

Each created in the year of the song release (from top to bottom, left to right)

Spadina

Classified and available through identifont.com

Design: i_dbuero × Sabine Schneider

let the music do the talking

3

DECEMBER

SONG
Let The Music Do The Talking
ARTIST
Aerosmith
YEAR
1980

SONGSPIRATION CONTEXT

Aerosmith guitarist Joe Perry wrote this song after leaving the band in 1979. He recorded it with his own group, The Joe Perry Project, making it the title track of their 1980 album. When Perry returned to Aerosmith in 1984, the band signed a new record deal with Geffen Records and began to sober up, leading to their wildly successful comeback. (songfacts.com)

FEATURED FONTS

Each created in the year of the song release (from top to bottom, left to right)

Belshaw

Classified and available through identifont.com

Design: i_dbuero × Sabine Schneider

you better do what you can

DECEMBER

SONG
Beat It
ARTIST
Michael Jackson
YEAR
1983

SONGSPIRATION CONTEXT

"I wanted to write a song, the type of song that I would buy if I were to buy a rock song ... That is how I approached it and I wanted the kids to really enjoy it—the school kids as well as the college kids."
(Michael Jackson)

FEATURED FONTS

Each created in the year of the song release (from top to bottom, left to right)

Delta BQ, Santa Fe

Classified and available through
identifont.com

Design: i_dbuero × Syl Hillier

There will never be ANOTHER YOU

DECEMBER

SONG
Never Be Another You

ARTIST
El Michels Affair & Lee Fields

YEAR
2018

SONGSPIRATION CONTEXT

On December 5, 1901, a little magic came into the world along with the birth of Walt Disney. He released his first cartoon, featuring Mickey Mouse, called *Steamboat Willie* at the age of 27. With his vision, Walt Disney made the whole world a happier place.

FEATURED FONTS

Each created in the year of the song release (from top to bottom, left to right)

Extenda

Classified and available through identifont.com

Design: i_dbuero × Carsten Güth

Perfect gifts.

www.seltmannpublishers.com

Worldwide shipping, free within Germany

You'll go down in hist...

SONG
Rudolph The Red-Nosed Reindeer

ARTIST
Johnny Marks

YEAR
1949

SONGSPIRATION CONTEXT
You know Dasher and Dancer and Prancer and Vixen, Comet and Cupid and Donner and Blitzen, but do you recall the most famous reindeer of them all? Of course you can remember the name of this famous even-toed ungulate. Happy St. Nicholas Day!

FEATURED FONTS
Each created in the year of the song release (from top to bottom, left to right)

Fairfield

Classified and available through identifont.com

Design: i_dbuero × OA Krimmel

Is there
anybody in there?

SONG
Comfortably Numb

ARTIST
Pink Floyd

YEAR
1979

SONGSPIRATION CONTEXT

Instead of 'Comfortably Numb', you could also feel pleasantly inspired at the moment. Start thinking about Christmas presents now. Personally selected music is always a fitting gift.

(Promotional advice: Also a great gift idea: the SONGSPIRATION calendar ;-))

FEATURED FONTS

Each created in the year of the song release (from top to bottom, left to right)

Glastonbury, OCR A

Classified and available through identifont.com

Design: i_dbuero × Carsten Güth

IMAGINE
all the
people
livin' life in
PEACE

SONG
Imagine
ARTIST
John Lennon
YEAR
1971

SONGSPIRATION CONTEXT

On the evening of 8 December 1980, English musician John Lennon, formerly of the Beatles, was shot and fatally wounded in the archway of *The Dakota*, his residence in New York City. His killer was Mark David Chapman, an American Beatles fan who was incensed by Lennon's lavish lifestyle and his 1966 comment that The Beatles were "more popular than Jesus". Chapman said he was inspired by the fictional character Holden Caulfield from J. D. Salinger's novel *The Catcher in the Rye*, a "phony-killer" who despises hypocrisy. (wikipedia)

FEATURED FONTS

Each created in the year of the song release (from top to bottom, left to right)

Jackson MN

Classified and available through
identifont.com

Design: i_dbuero × Sabine Schneider

AH, FREAK OUT!

DECEMBER

SONG
Le Freak
ARTIST
Chic
YEAR
1978

SONGSPIRATION CONTEXT

The band “Chic” had been invited by singer Grace Jones to the New Year’s Eve ‘77 party at the famous Studio 54 in New York, but were not on the guest list. The tough bouncers didn’t believe them and turned them away with the words “Fuck off”. Pissed off, the band returned to their studio and vented their frustration, chanting “Fuck off - Fuck Studio 54” to an improvised riff. Since they immediately liked the sound and the melody, they changed the lyrics and made it “Ah, freak out - Le freak, c’est chic”.

FEATURED FONTS

Each created in the year of the song release (from top to bottom, left to right)

Croissant

Classified and available through identifont.com

Design: i_dbuero × Carsten Güth

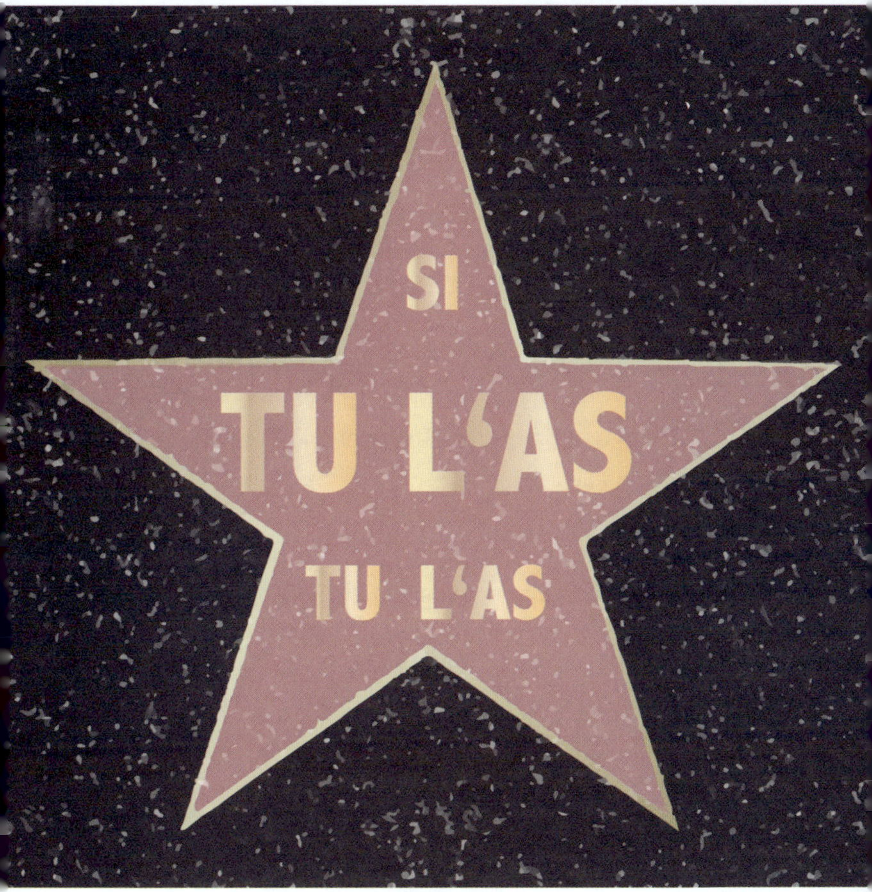

SI

TU L'AS

TU L'AS

DECEMBER

SONG
Ella, elle l'a
ARTIST
France Gall
YEAR
1987

SONGSPIRATION CONTEXT

The song lyrics, which the husband of France Gall, composer Michel Berger, had already begun a decade earlier, is a tribute to the world-famous singer Ella Fitzgerald. On this day in 1947, she married the bassist Ray Brown. "Lady Ella" has had her own Star on the Hollywood Walk of Fame since 1960.

FEATURED FONTS

Each created in the year of the song release (from top to bottom, left to right)

Abadi

Classified and available through
identifont.com

Design: i_dbuero × OA Krimmel
Celebrating: Ella-Ray

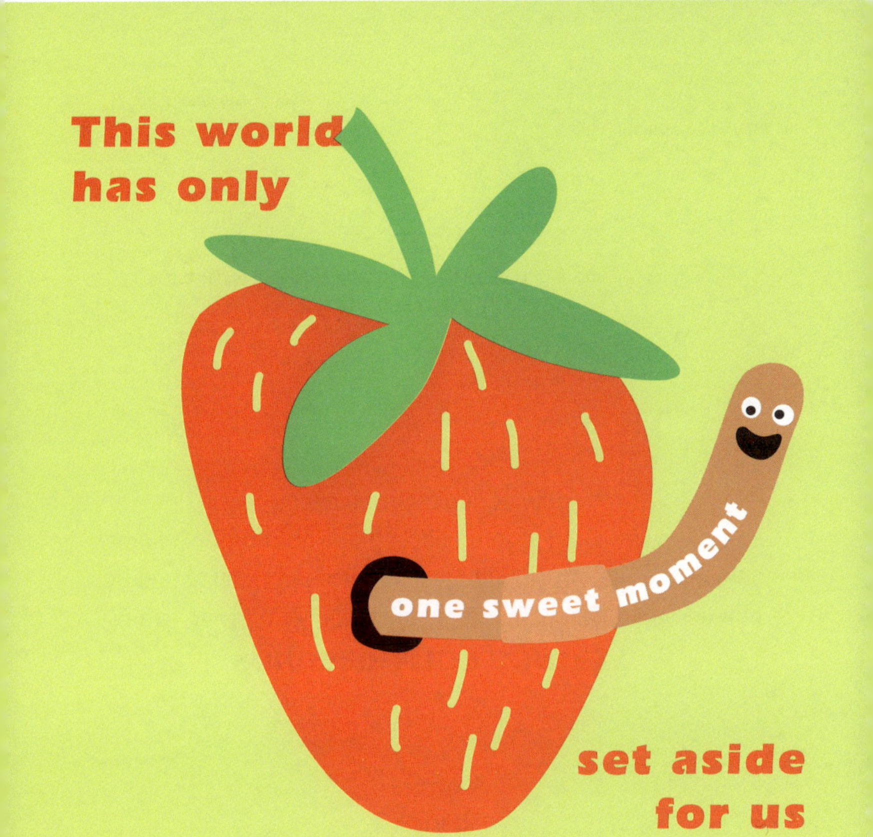

This world has only

one sweet moment

set aside for us

DECEMBER

SONG
Who Wants to Live Forever
ARTIST
Queen
YEAR
1986

SONGSPIRATION CONTEXT

On this day in 1972, *Apollo 17* astronauts Eugene Cernan and Harrison Schmitt became the last humans to walk on the Moon and on YouTube you'll find video proof of them being the first humans to sing on the Moon.

FEATURED FONTS

Each created in the year of the song release (from top to bottom, left to right)

ITC Eras

Classified and available through identifont.com

Design: i_dbuero × Evelyn Binder

12

DECEMBER

SONG
Jump
ARTIST
Madonna
YEAR
2005

SONGSPIRATION CONTEXT

On December 12, 1996, Madonna attended a press conference to promote *EVITA* at the Ritz-Carlton Hotel in Marina Del Rey, California. It wasn't the first time Madonna was ready to jump into the movie business and we're pretty sure she'll look back fondly on this picture.

FEATURED FONTS

Each created in the year of the song release (from top to bottom, left to right)

Chaser, Liana

Classified and available through identifont.com

Design: i_dbuero × Syl Hillier

13

DECEMBER

SONG
Love Is a Battlefield
ARTIST
Pat Benatar
YEAR
1983

SONGSPIRATION CONTEXT

13, the magic number. This song plays a big role in the 2004 movie *13 Going on 30*, where "love is a battlefield" is Jennifer Garner's mantra. Garner, who becomes a 13-year-old from the '80s transformed into a 30-year-old, sings it with some young girls she is helping to learn about love.

FEATURED FONTS

Each created in the year of the song release (from top to bottom, left to right)

Julia Script

Classified and available through identifont.com

Design: i_dbuero × Sabine Schneider

WE'RE JUST
TWO
LOST SOULS
SWIMMING
IN A FISHBOWL
YEAR AFTER
YEAR

SONG
Wish You Were Here
ARTIST
Pink Floyd
YEAR
1975

SONGSPIRATION CONTEXT

At no time did Amundsen and Scott acknowledge or plan for a race, they both planned expeditions with the ambition to be the first man to reach one of the last great geographic goals of the age, the South Pole. But at l(e)ast on this day in 1911, Roald Amundsen became the first person to reach the South Pole.

FEATURED FONTS

Each created in the year of the song release (from top to bottom, left to right)

Buxom D

Classified and available through identifont.com

Design: i_dbuero × Sabine Schneider

I want it hot

hot, hot

and then terribly

cold, cold

SONG
Hot Hot Cold Cold
ARTIST
Oum Shatt
YEAR
2014

SONGSPIRATION CONTEXT

The onomatopoeic band name is quite sonorous. It is a homage to the influential Egyptian singer Oum Kulthoum. Her fame in the Arab world is comparable to that of Maria Callas and The Beatles in the Western world. In their music, the band repeatedly sprinkles references to Arabic and Turkish melodies.

FEATURED FONTS

Each created in the year of the song release (from top to bottom, left to right)

BB Book

Classified and available through
identifont.com

Design: i_dbuero × Carsten Güth

Most days in life don't stand out, but life's about those days that will

SONG
Talladega
ARTIST
Eric Church
YEAR
2006

SONGSPIRATION CONTEXT

The Boston Tea Party was a political protest that occurred on December 16, 1773, at Griffin's Wharf in Boston, Massachusetts. American colonists, frustrated and angry at Britain for imposing "taxation without representation," dumped 342 chests of tea, imported by the British East India Company into the harbor.

FEATURED FONTS

Each created in the year of the song release (from top to bottom, left to right)

Fakir

Classified and available through identifont.com

Design: i_dbuero × Carsten Güth

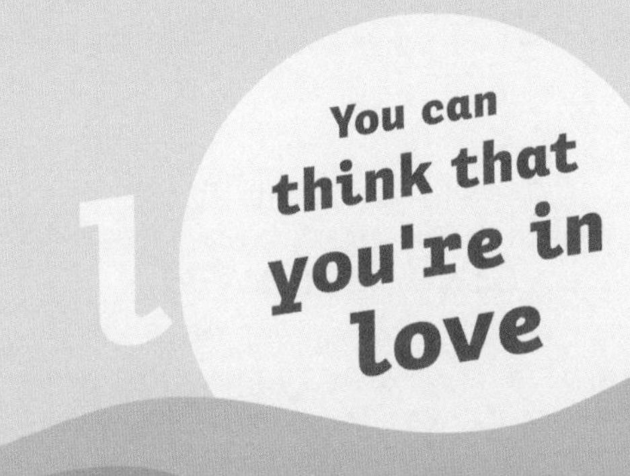

when you're really just in pain

17 DECEMBER

SONG
Moral Of The Story
ARTIST
Ashe
YEAR
2020

SONGSPIRATION CONTEXT

"It's hard to accept when you've made a mistake in love or life. But realizing all those mistakes have made you who you are and have helped shape the life you're in you puts a different light on things."
("Ashe" Ashlyn Rae Willson)

FEATURED FONTS

Each created in the year of the song release (from top to bottom, left to right)

Adelle Mono Flex

Classified and available through identifont.com

Design: i_dbuero × OA Krimmel

IT'S FOUR
IN THE MORNING,
THE END OF
DECEMBER

SONG
Famous Blue Raincoat
ARTIST
Leonard Cohen
YEAR
1971

SONGSPIRATION CONTEXT

A great artist can create a touching song out of anything. Well, Leonard Cohen can anyway. He “simply” sings a written letter to a friend in which a “famous blue raincoat” appears. The song ends quite coherently, just like his letter: “Sincerely L. Cohen”.

FEATURED FONTS

Each created in the year of the song release (from top to bottom, left to right)

Sackers Gothic

Classified and available through identifont.com

Design: i_dbuero × Carsten Güth

IF YOU
LEAVE
ME NOW
YOU'LL
TAKE
AWAY
THE
BIGGEST
PART
OF ME

SONG
If you leave me now

ARTIST
Chicago

YEAR
1977

SONGSPIRATION CONTEXT
In fact, today is the 353rd day of the year (354th day in leap years). There are only 12 days left until the end of the year. And "the biggest part of me", your SONGSPIRATION calendar you have already taken away. Well so, have fun with the final spurt ...

FEATURED FONTS
Each created in the year of the song release (from top to bottom, left to right)

Caslon

Classified and available through identifont.com

Design: i_dbuero × Carsten Güth

sometimes
I wanna
KEEP
YOU
WARM
sometimes
I wanna
wrap my coat
around you

SONG
Winter
ARTIST
The Rolling Stones
YEAR
1973

SONGSPIRATION CONTEXT

December 20, 1969: The Stones went to No. 1 on the UK album chart with the *Let It Bleed* album.
Since then, the Rolling Stones have released almost 100 albums to "keep us warm".

FEATURED FONTS

Each created in the year of the song release (from top to bottom, left to right)

Stilla

Classified and available through identifont.com

Design: i_dbuero × Sabine Schneider

Je t'aime,

je t'aime

SONG
Je t'aime moi non plus

ARTIST
Brigitte Bardot & Serge Gainsbourg

YEAR
1967

SONGSPIRATION CONTEXT

Today we celebrate World Orgasm Day. The appropriate song is undoubtedly "Je t'aime" . The first version is by Brigitte Bardot with Serge Gainsbourg – but her then husband, the playboy Gunter Sachs had the version jealously banned at first, two years later Gainsbourg recorded the whole thing with his mistress Jane Birkin and the sung sex went around the world.

FEATURED FONTS

Each created in the year of the song release (from top to bottom, left to right)

Ecsetiras, Egyptian 505

Classified and available through identifont.com

Design: i_dbuero × Syl Hillier

Only a hippopotamus will do

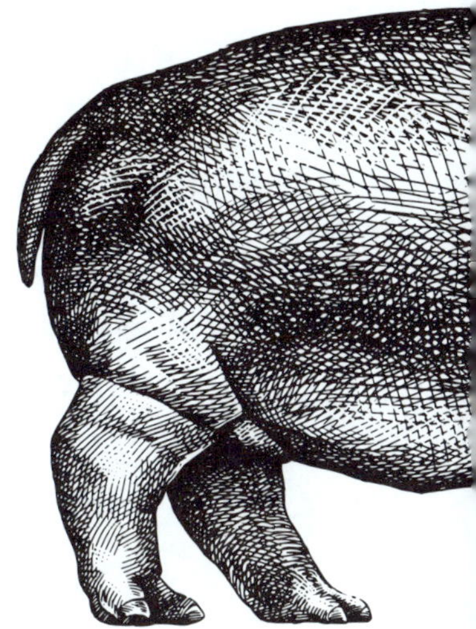

SONG
I Want A Hippopotamus For Christmas
ARTIST
Gayla Peevey
YEAR
1953

SONGSPIRATION CONTEXT
This song was originally sung by a 10-year-old girl in 1953 in Oklahoma to raise money so that the Oklahoma Zoo could get their first hippopotamus. Of course, after this happened it became a huge hit throughout the country.

FEATURED FONTS
Each created in the year of the song release (from top to bottom, left to right)

Clarendon Heavy

Classified and available through identifont.com

Design: i_dbuero × OA Krimmel

I can feel it coming in the Air tonight.

SONG
In The Air Tonight
ARTIST
Phil Collins
YEAR
1981

SONGSPIRATION CONTEXT

Before the ice is in the pools / Before the skaters go, /
Or any check at nightfall / Is tarnished by the snow /
Before the fields have finished, / Before the Christmas tree, /
Wonder upon wonder / Will arrive to me! (Emily Dickinson)

FEATURED FONTS

Each created in the year of the song release (from top to bottom, left to right)

Aja, Corinthian, ITC Barcelona

Classified and available through
identifont.com

Design: i_dbuero × Carsten Güth

you
CAN'T
always
GET WHAT
YOU
want

24

DECEMBER

SONG
You Can't Always Get What You Want

ARTIST
The Rolling Stones

YEAR
1969

SONGSPIRATION CONTEXT
"Merry Christmas, Happy Holidays and a Happy New Year to you all!" (@mickjagger)

FEATURED FONTS
Each created in the year of the song release (from top to bottom, left to right)

Aachen, Didoni

Classified and available through identifont.com

Design: i_dbuero × Carsten Güth

BUT IF YOU
TRY SOMETIMES
WELL, YOU'LL FIND

you get
what
you
need

DECEMBER

SONG
You Can‘t Always Get What You Want

ARTIST
The Rolling Stones

YEAR
1969

SONGSPIRATION CONTEXT
“But if you try sometimes you just might find, uh, mm
You get what you need, oh yeah, woo! Ah, woo!”

FEATURED FONTS
Each created in the year of the song release (from top to bottom, left to right)

Aachen, Didoni

Classified and available through
identifont.com

Design: i_dbuero × Carsten Güth

WAR

So this

IS

Chr tmas

OVER!

IF YOU WANT IT

DECEMBER

SONG
Happy XMas (War Is Over)
ARTIST
John Lennon & Yoko Ono
YEAR
1971

SONGSPIRATION CONTEXT

"Yoko and I wrote 'Happy Xmas' together. It says: 'War is over if you want it'. That was still the same message – the idea that we are just as responsible as the man pushing the buttons. As long as people have the idea that somebody is doing it to them and that they have no power, they have no power." (John Lennon)

FEATURED FONTS

Each created in the year of the song release (from top to bottom, left to right)

Lapture, Franklin Gothic

Classified and available through identifont.com

Design: i_dbuero × Sarah Meßelken

Don't worry where we end up

27

DECEMBER

SONG
Delivery

ARTIST
Jimmy Eat World

YEAR
2019

SONGSPIRATION CONTEXT

The band's name comes from a drawing Tom Linton's younger brother Ed drew when he was eight years old. After an altercation with his overweight brother Jim, Ed titled the drawing 'Jimmy Eat World' as a way to say that his brother was so fat he could eat the whole world.

FEATURED FONTS

Each created in the year of the song release (from top to bottom, left to right)

Blackest

Classified and available through identifont.com

Design: i_dbuero × Carsten Güth

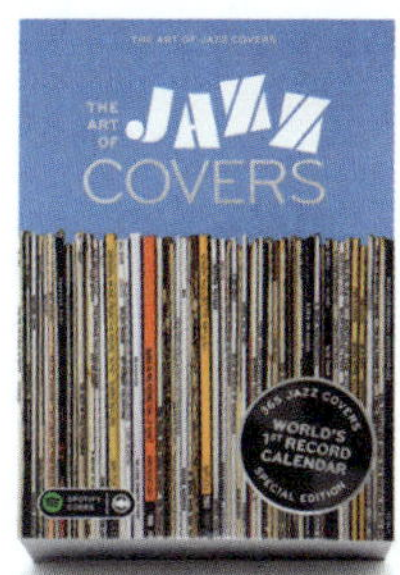

www.seltmannpublishers.com

Worldwide shipping, free within Germany

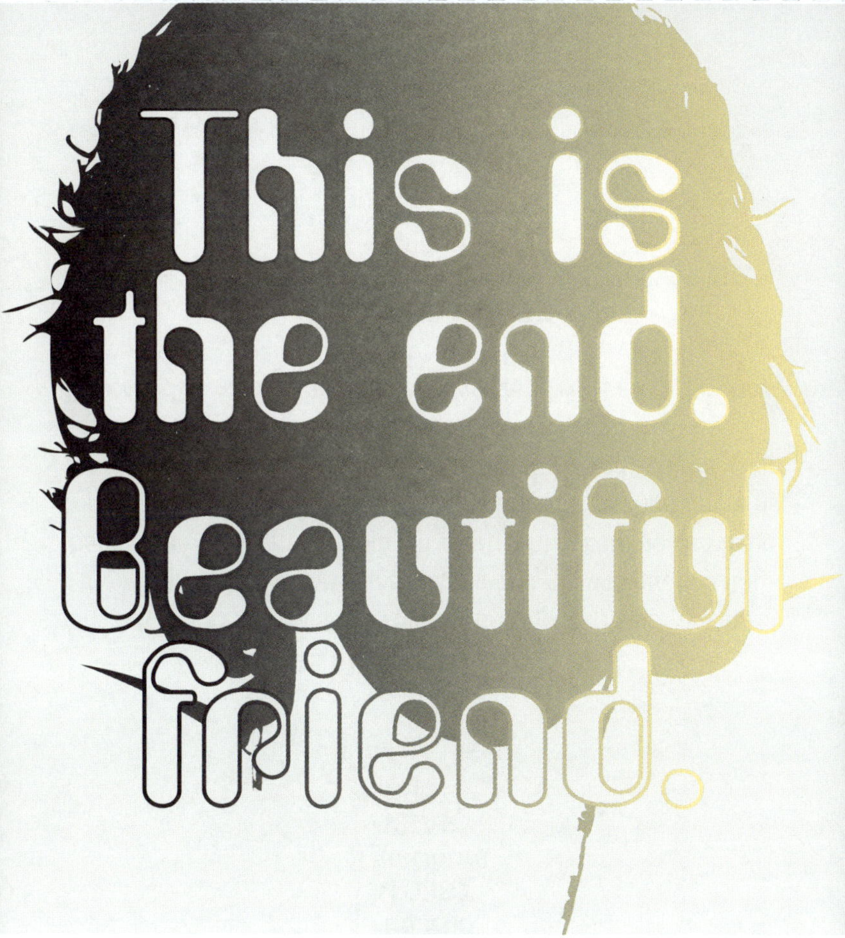

This is the end. Beautiful friend.

DECEMBER

SONG
The End
ARTIST
The Doors
YEAR
1967

SONGSPIRATION CONTEXT

One day in 1966 Jim Morrison didn't show up for The Doors gig at the Whisky a Go Go. After playing the first set without him, the band retrieved Morrison from his apartment, where he had been tripping on acid. When they got to the part of "The End" where he could do a spoken improvisation, he started talking about a killer, and said, "Father, I want to kill you. Mother, I want to f--k you!" The crowd went nuts, but the band was fired right after the show.

FEATURED FONTS

Each created in the year of the song release (from top to bottom, left to right)

Amelia

Classified and available through identifont.com

Design: i_dbuero × Sabine Schneider

Music was my first Love & it will be my Last

SONG
Music Was My First Love

ARTIST
John Miles

YEAR
1976

SONGSPIRATION CONTEXT
This song title is a life essence.
That's why this calendar page is the only one that appears twice in this calendar :)

FEATURED FONTS
Each created in the year of the song release (from top to bottom, left to right)

Bogart

Classified and available through identifont.com

Design: i_dbuero × Carsten Güth

YOU

READY?

DECEMBER

SONG
SexyBack
ARTIST
Justin Timberlake
YEAR
2006

SONGSPIRATION CONTEXT

What are YOUR top 3 New Year's resolutions?

SONGSPIRATION'S tip: Just add 'more dancing' to it ...

FEATURED FONTS

Each created in the year of the song release (from top to bottom, left to right)

Blender Pro

Classified and available through identifont.com

Design: i_dbuero × OA Krimmel

098 1T'S 765

210 7HE 1098

54 F1N4L 321

98 COUN7- 76

210 DOWN 10

31

DECEMBER

SONG
The Final Countdown
ARTIST
Europe
YEAR
1986

SONGSPIRATION CONTEXT

We wish you all the best,
may you have a wonderful year ahead ...

(P.S. Don't forget about your top 3 New Year's resolutions from yesterday.)
Goodbye.

FEATURED FONTS

Each created in the year of the song release (from top to bottom, left to right)

Citizen

Classified and available through identifont.com

Design: i_dbuero × Carsten Güth

THANKS TO THE FOUNDRIES & DEVELOPERS & DESIGNERS

Thanks to the committed teams of IDENTIFONT and SELTMANN PUBLISHERS.

Special thanks to Dough Shaw, MONOTYPE, Charles Ying (R.I.P), MYFONTS, and David Johnson-Davies, IDENTIFONT for paving the way for this project.

The fonts used in this calendar have been licensed either by the respective designers, i_dbuero, the publisher, ADOBE FONTS or the Bitstream Typeface Library of the State Academy of Fine Arts Stuttgart for the present purpose of use. We would like to thank the font designers and font libraries, illustrators and text sources that provided us with their content free of charge. Also thanks go out to the online distributors and creators of font bundles.
We have made every effort to locate all rights holders, to name and honor them as is customary with publishers.
Should this not have been possible in individual cases, please may the copyright holder inform us.

Insofar as this publication contains links to third-party websites, we assume no liability for their contents, as we do not adopt them as our own, but merely refer to their status at the time of initial publication.

IMPRINT
SONGSPIRATION

3. unveränderte Auflage

Seltmann Publishers
Berlin, Germany
www.seltmannpublishers.com
info@seltmannpublishers.de

Concept & Text:
OA Krimmel,
Stuttgart, Germany

@songspiration365

All Artworks © i_d buero *All-Stars*

Creative Direction: OA Krimmel / i_d buero
Special thanks to Carsten, Sabine, Hanna, Evelyn & Anja

All rights reserved.
This calendar may not be reproduced in whole or in part, stored in a retrieval system, or processed by electronic mechanical means, photo-copying, recording or otherwise, without the prior written consent of the copyright owner.

© 2023 / 2025 Seltmann Publishers

ISBN 978-3-949070-17-4

THANKS TO THE
ALL-STARS-TEAM OF I_D BUERO

Great to have had you here!

Pia **B**ardesono, Dörte Bicker, Evelyn Binder, Daniel Bognár, Nicole Borbely, Silke Braun, Kitty **C**arrera, Christine **D**orst, Martin Drozmann, Peggy Durweiler, Caroline **G**lock, Carsten Güth, Syl **H**illier, Hannah Hoffmann, Thomas Hofmann, Jan Hurni, Robert **J**ähnigen, Hojin **K**ang, OA Krimmel, Dennis Kulbe, Jan **M**aier, Sarah Messelken, Silke Mennenga, Jan Michalski, Kristin Munz, Anja **O**sterwalder, Anna-Maria **P**aschetto, Björn Börris Peters, Nils Prenz, Ralph **R**ieker, Jochen **S**chieborn, Sabine Schneider, Katrin Schlüsener, Tim Oliver Schweizer, Hanna Spitznagel, Jana Steffen, James **T**ucker, Susanne **W**agner, Frank **Z**uber &
Alexandra, Anna, Claudia, Stefan, Susanna, Thors10, Petroula & X.
also Christoph Binder, Sarah Grgic, Mavi Schuler